GREEK MYTHS

Retold by Jacqueline Morley
Illustrated by Giovanni Caselli

PETER BEDRICK BOOKS
NEW YORK

Published by
PETER BEDRICK BOOKS
a division of NTC/Contemporary Publishing Group, Inc.
4255 West Touhy Avenue, Lincolnwood (Chicago)
Illinois 60712-1975

Library of Congress Cataloging-in-Publication Data
Morley, Jacqueline.
Greek myths / retold by Jacqueline Morley : Illustrated by Giovanni Caselli.
        p.   cm.
Includes index.
Summary: An illustrated collection of twenty Greek myths including
"Prometheus and Pandora," "Theseus and the Minotaur,"
"Meleager and the blazing logs," and "The story of Phaeton."
ISBN 0-87226-560-9
1. Mythology, Greek—Juvenile literature. [1. Mythology, Greek.]
I. Caselli, Giovanni, 1939-   ill. II. Title.
BL782.M67 1998
398.2'0938'01—dc21
97–45899
CIP AC

Designed by Dalia Hartman
Typeset in Garland Light
Printed and bound by Asa, Portugal
First Printing, 1998
Second Printing, 1999

CONTENTS

INTRODUCTION

Myths are the world's oldest stories. All peoples have them; they are our earliest attempts to make sense of life. A myth differs from a legend, which tells of marvellous happenings in the distant past, for the events of a myth take place outside historical time. Myths were the earliest explanations of the world: How did we get here? Who made us? Why do we live by certain rules? What happens when we die? The answers took the form of stories of gods and goddesses, monsters and demons. More than any other myths of the Western world, those of the ancient Greeks have kept their hold over people's imaginations. We meet their stories again and again, in literature, music, painting and architecture.

For the ancient Greeks who created them, the myths were sacred stories - the equivalent of the Bible stories for Jewish or Christian believers. And like the Old Testament stories, they were first written down by writers who were primarily poets. In the eighth century BC, the Greek poet Hesiod recorded the stories, already very old, of the origin of the gods and the making of the world, and Homer, in his great poems the Iliad and the Odyssey, told of the Trojan war and the adventures of Odysseus. In the fifth century BC, Aeschylus, Sophocles and Euripides, the creators of tragic drama, interpreted many of the stories in their plays. The later Greeks and Romans retold them; especially famous are the poems of the Roman poet Ovid, written at around the start of the Christian era. These writers gave the ancient tales such powerful expression that they have outlived the beliefs they served by almost two thousand years, and inspired writers and artists who no longer accepted their religious truth.

An inkling of what the stories meant to the Greeks helps to explain their strange power. Myths are not fairy stories, in which good characters end up happy and wicked stepmothers are punished. Myths tell of gods and heroes who are neither good nor bad, and of doings which seem cruel, unexplained, unfair. Zeus, the king of the gods, enforced law and order in the world but was himself unpredictable and vengeful (we might consider him a bad husband too, but to the ancient Greeks Zeus's many loves were an aspect of his power). Even Athene, the wisest of the goddesses, in one story has a fit of jealous rage. The wilfulness of the gods reflected the uncertainties of life. The ancient Greeks believed in them and honoured them, but knew that their kindness could not be relied on and that they could be unjust. For how else could people's misfortunes be explained?

By the time the Romans had conquered the Greeks, the old myths were regarded much more lightly, and the re-tellings by Ovid embroidered them with fanciful detail so that they took a step towards being merely the beautiful and evocative stories that they became for the Middle Ages and the Renaissance. For unlike the writings of many Greek and Latin authors, the works of Ovid were never lost, and because the medieval Church carried on using Latin, people could still read the myths. They prompted some of the most beautiful literature, music and paintings of the Renaissance, and have continued to inspire artists and musicians to the present day.

Closely intertwined with the earliest myths of the gods are the stories of the heroes. The term hero meant not just a brave person, but one of the legendary godlike mortals, often fathered by a god, who did great deeds on earth. Some of the most famous stories - the Gorgon's Head, the Golden Fleece, the Wooden Horse - are of the heroes. Choosing only twenty stories of Greek gods and heroes has been a hard task. Some tucks have been made in the telling and some characters missed out, but the heart of each story is here. I hope when you have finished this book you will hunt for others, to discover more about the Argonauts' adventures, the perils Theseus met on his way to join his father, how Jason met his death - there is so much more than I have been able to tell.

Jacqueline Morley 1997

PROMETHEUS AND PANDORA

This is the story of how the world began, as the ancient Greeks told it.

The first thing that existed, the oldest thing of all, was chaos. No one can say what chaos looked like. It had no height, or width or depth, yet it was everywhere. And out of chaos Mother Earth emerged. Her name was Gaia. Gaia created the mountains, the plains, the rivers and the foaming seas. Then she took a husband - Uranus, the starry sky - and poured forth living creatures, the lion, the horse, the eagle and all the birds and beasts we know today. But others that she made were strange and monstrous, giants with a hundred arms or one eye in their forehead, and nymphs, the female spirits of the woods and waters. Then Gaia bore the first rulers of the earth, six sons and six daughters - the Titans.

The Titans were like their mother - strong and lawless. Cronus, their ruler, ate his children as soon as they were born, for Gaia had warned him that a powerful son would overthrow him. His precautions were useless, for not even the gods can escape their fate. It was the destiny of the Titans to be defeated by younger, nobler gods. Cronus's wife Rhea outwitted her hated husband. She hid her sixth child, a boy named Zeus, in a cave, and offered Cronus a great stone swaddled like a baby to eat instead. Cronus thrust the stone into his stomach, never dreaming that he had a son alive, cared for by the nymphs and growing stronger by the day.

One day Rhea said to Cronus 'I have got rid of that useless creature that serves you at table. This is your new cupbearer.' The new attendant, who looked tall and powerful, offered Cronus a honeyed drink. Cronus gulped it down and at once felt drowsy and rather ill. As he slid into irresistible sleep, he realized, in a befuddled way, that he had been tricked. The cupbearer was his son Zeus, who had given him a herb to make him vomit violently in his sleep. Out came the stone he had swallowed, followed

7

by Zeus's elder brothers and sisters, who sprang out quite unhurt. They bound their father with chains and declared Zeus master of the world.

Zeus cast the Titans to the outer ends of the earth and compelled Atlas, the brawniest, to support the sky upon his shoulders for ever. The new gods made their home on the top of lofty Mount Olympus. From his palace high above the clouds Zeus kept an eye on what went on below. His brow grew very black when he discovered the Titans befriending some creatures that were new on earth - mortal beings called men.

Some say that Mother Earth had made men spring from the rocks and soil. Others say a Titan called Prometheus took potter's clay and modelled them. Prometheus was clever, a maker of things who taught men

skills when they were new to the world. Mother Earth gave him an enormous basket of gifts and told him to share them out among all mortal creatures. 'I have made them too hastily,' she said, 'and life is hard for them.'

Now Prometheus had a brother called Epimetheus who was as foolish as Prometheus was wise. When Epimetheus saw the basket he begged to be allowed to do the sharing.

'Certainly not' said Prometheus. 'You'll make a mess of it.'

But Epimetheus pleaded so much that Prometheus agreed he could start giving away the small gifts. Epimetheus gave a shell to the crab, fangs to the snake, long legs to the hare, and so on. He soon came to the end of the smaller things. Then he gave swift wings to the eagle and ferocity to the lion, and so delighted them that he could not stop. When

Prometheus returned the basket was empty.

'You didn't think I'd manage,' said Epimetheus triumphantly 'but I've done a perfect job. There was just enough to go round.' 'What did you give to men?' asked Prometheus sharply.

Epimetheus had to admit he had quite forgotten about men. Prometheus was furious, chiefly with himself for letting this happen. Men needed a gift so he decided to fetch them fire from heaven.

Now Zeus had a poor opinion of mankind, whom he suspected of plotting with the Titans. To keep men helpless, he had hidden fire on Olympus and meant to keep it from them. 'They can eat raw meat, and shiver' he said. Prometheus crept up to Olympus, into the forge of Hephaestus the god of fire, and smuggled out a glowing ember hidden in a hollow fennel stalk. From it he lit a torch and brought it flaming down from heaven to men.

This was the best gift he could have given them. With fire they had warmth and light and could forge tools to build houses and make ploughs. But Zeus was angry and revengeful. He called the gods to him and said in a deceptively mild way, 'Men are lonely in the world so I have made a companion for them – woman.' He showed them a lovely creature like a goddess. 'I have done my best,' he said 'Now each of you must give her a gift and she will be perfect – our present to mankind.' So Aphrodite, goddess of love, gave her beauty; Hermes, the gods' quick-silver messenger, filled her with liveliness and cunning; the Graces gave

her irresistible charm. Each god gave something, and she was named Pandora, which means 'all gifts', because nothing was omitted that could win men's hearts.

Zeus then commanded Hermes the messenger to lead Pandora down to earth. But at the last minute he called them back. 'This is for you' he said and he gave Pandora a box. 'But see that you never open it' he added, and smiled secretly.

Hermes brought Pandora to Prometheus, but he was suspicious and refused to have anything to do with her. Soft-hearted Epimetheus said, 'I'll look after her.'

'Don't,' Prometheus told him. 'You are a fool, Epimetheus. No good will come of anything from Zeus.'

Epimetheus did not listen. He took Pandora home and the two lived contentedly for a time. Then Pandora became restless.

'I can't think why Zeus gave me that box,' she kept saying.

'Neither can I' Epimetheus would reply without much interest.

'He told me not to look in it.'

'Then we needn't bother about it, need we, Pandora?'

But Pandora could not leave it at that. She thought that Epimetheus was stupid to show so little curiosity. 'I'll take just one peep,' she thought. She undid the clasp.

Immediately the lid flew open and a swarm of hideous mischiefs and misfortunes shot into the air – envy and greed and sickness and old age, famine and war, deceit, lies, fear, and useless pride. Pandora shrieked as the horrid things rushed past her face and flew into the open air, scattering far and wide throughout the world, where they have been tormenting people ever since. It was too late now to close the box. There was only one thing left in it, a tiny flame that flickered as if at any moment it would go out. This too rose in the air and followed the rest. This flame was Hope. Zeus's heart had softened sufficiently to allow mankind this one comfort, which has helped it to endure a thousand ills.

THE STORY OF PERSEPHONE

In the beginning of time, there was no winter. Every day the sun shone and showers lasted only long enough to make a rainbow. Trees had leaves all year round, and bore fruit and flowers together. After defeating the Titans the three most powerful gods of Olympus drew lots to decide how to share out this fresh new world between them. They shook the lots in a helmet and each god drew the lot that suited him best. Zeus, the mightiest of the gods, became lord of the earth and sky and ruled them with his thunderbolts. His brother, blustery Poseidon, won the seas and took delight in making floods and gales. The third brother, gloomy and morose Hades, became king of the underworld – land of the dead.

From his underground kingdom, Hades looked enviously at the world above. He was pleased to rule the shadows whose earthly life was over, for his subjects could never escape. 'There are no rebels in my kingdom,' he boasted grimly. But he dearly longed for a little of life's warmth to cheer his icy palace. He had seen on earth a young girl so beautiful that she outshone everyone, yet so happy that she was never without companions. Her name was Persephone. Hades wanted her as his queen.

Mounting his chariot, drawn by black horses, Hades rode to Mount Olympus and demanded that Zeus should give him Persephone as his bride. Zeus was cautious. He could not please Hades without angering Persephone's mother, the powerful goddess Demeter who caused all living things to grow. She made seeds sprout and blossom open and fruits swell. The thought of her daughter living in the dim underworld would be hateful to her.

So Zeus's answer was diplomatic. 'That might be an excellent idea,' he said, 'a little later on.'

For several days Hades sat brooding on his iron throne. Then he leapt into his chariot and rode his black horses out of the earth and snatched up

Persephone as she was gathering wild flowers in a meadow. He galloped away with her and the earth closed over them. Her companions heard her shrieks and came running, but they could find no trace of her, nothing but a bunch of flowers she had let fall on the grass.

When Demeter learned that her daughter had vanished, she wrapped herself in a long dark cloak and went out into the world to look for her. She wandered for nine days and nights, asking every living creature for news of Persephone. No one had seen her. She was returning weary and heartbroken when she saw a piece of ribbon in a deep cleft among the grass. It was Persephone's girdle. Not knowing what this could mean, but full of dread, she sank down upon a stone and wept. Then Helios, the god who drives the sun across the sky, came to her at nightfall and told her that from his chariot he had seen Persephone carried off by Hades to be queen of the underworld.

Then Demeter's sorrow turned to terrible rage. She vowed that nothing should grow on earth until her daughter was given back to her. No one could make the angry goddess change her mind. When farmers sowed their fields the seed rotted in the ground; the stems of plants withered and the trees lost their leaves; fruits shrivelled and the corn grew mildewed. The people of the earth were in despair and starving. They blamed the gods and harassed them with never-ending prayers to put things right. Zeus saw that he must take action. He sent his son Hermes, the silver-tongued messenger of the gods, to plead with Hades.

Hermes was the only god likely to talk Hades into parting with his bride. Though the gods' messenger was as nimble as the air through which he darted on winged sandals, his wits were nimbler still. Humbly, and with a charming smile, he presented himself before Hades who sat enthroned with pale-lipped Persephone by his side. She seemed a shadow of herself for, despite Hades' coaxing, she had refused to eat a morsel since he had brought her there.

'Great lord,' began Hermes, 'the gods of Olympus are impressed by the changes you have brought about in the world.'

'The people are all dying' agreed Hades calmly, 'and then they come to me.'

'And when all are dead?' said Hermes. 'How will your empire grow when there are no new souls to swell it? Have pity on the world. Think of the future and let Persephone go.'

Hades gave him a long look, and then sighed as if his heart were broken. 'Take her,' he said, 'and I will rule alone.'

Joyfully Hermes led Persephone back to the day. Demeter flung her arms round her daughter to kiss her, but then she drew back in alarm. She had felt the cold touch of the underworld upon her daughter's cheek. 'Did you eat anything in Hades' kingdom? she asked her anxiously.

'Nothing, mother,' Persephone replied. 'But I was so thirsty that Hades gave me a pomegranate to suck and I swallowed seven of its seeds.'

Then Demeter knew that Hades had tricked her, for no one who eats the food of the dead can escape the underworld.

Even all-powerful Zeus could not alter this law but he made Hades accept a compromise. For half of each year Persephone must reign in the underworld. Then Demeter's sorrow makes the earth grow cold; leaves fall and plants hide in the soil; winter comes. But for the rest of the year Persephone is restored to her mother, the first flowers appear and spring returns. Demeter forgets her grief, and the earth teems with life again.

THE STORY OF ARACHNE

The Olympian gods were kind to mortals when it suited them. When Prometheus made the first men out of clay the poor creatures had little idea how to look after themselves. So the gods stepped in to help them. Demeter showed them how to plant corn and grow food. Hephaestus, god of fire, taught them to cast metal and become craftsmen. Athene, the wisest of the gods, gave them the olive, the most useful of all trees, and taught them cooking, weaving and spinning, the skills that make life comfortable and pleasant. In return for being so obliging the gods expected gratitude. They wanted temples to be built to them and offerings put upon their altars. They liked constant praise, and if they did not get it their anger could be terrible. If anyone spoke scornfully of the gods, someone was sure to say, 'Remember what happened to Arachne.'

Everyone had heard of Arachne, though in fact she was an ordinary girl. She was not beautiful, or rich, or particularly clever, but she was nimble-fingered. No one could spin thread faster then Arachne, or make it so supple and fine. 'If only we could do work like Arachne's,' her friends sighed. For in those days, when cloth was made by hand, all girls had to spin and weave.

'You need to have hands like mine,' said Arachne, spreading out her long, slender fingers and admiring them. 'I don't think anyone has such a quick, light touch as I have.'

And with the airy yarn she spun, Arachne wove cloth that was a miracle of loveliness - gossamer fine fabrics and patterned tapestries, with scenes of trees and birds and sky and sun and stars, fit for the walls of a king's palace. Wood nymphs left their forests and river nymphs came dripping from their streams to watch her as she sent the shuttle flying back and forth across the loom. The threads seemed to dance into place of their own accord. The nymphs would lean forward to touch the woven leaves and flowers and exclaim, 'Arachne, you could charm the birds out of the sky to visit trees like these!'

'You have to judge the colours and effects' said Arachne. 'I don't think anyone has such an eye for pattern as myself.'

No one dreamed of contradicting her. Everyone praised Arachne. 'You can see that Athene herself has taught her' said a friend.

'Athene!' scowled Arachne. 'She couldn't teach me anything. A born artist doesn't need a tutor. Athene would be in a tight corner if she had to compete with me.'

An old woman wrapped in a grey cloak had been standing in the doorway among the crowd that always gathered while Arachne worked. Now she came forward shaking her stick at her. 'You are a bold one, boasting of being better than the gods', she croaked. 'If you'd take the advice of an old woman, you'd beg Athene to forget your words.'

'I wouldn't beg Athene for a bodkin' retorted Arachne. 'Keep your advice for your grandchildren – if they want it. I don't need some dim-eyed old woman to tell me what to do.'

Then that old woman grew tall and straight and threw off her cloak. It was the goddess herself. Her glance was terrifying. The onlookers, women and nymphs, bowed to the ground in fear. Even Arachne leapt up from her loom and seemed about to drop to her knees, but she quickly recovered herself. 'If I have spoken hastily' she said 'I

have done wrong. But let our work prove whether I have spoken falsely.'

'You dare to challenge me!' exclaimed Athene. 'Then I accept the challenge.'

Then the tall goddess and the young woman set up their looms, one on each side of the room, and began to weave. News of the contest spread with the speed of fire, and people crowded into Arachne's cottage to watch the work, though none dared press too closely round the goddess. Athene tucked the long folds of her gown into her girdle, to keep them out of the way, and bent her golden head close to her work. Her tapestry, in rainbow threads and gold and silver, seemed to unfold beneath her hands upon the loom. After a while she laid down her boxwood shuttle and gave her work an approving look. Then she turned to see what her rival had been doing.

The onlookers round Arachne's loom were silent and seemed embarassed. When Athene saw the glimmering scenes upon the loom her eyebrows met in a dark line of fury. Arachne's tapestry showed stories of the gods, not in their glorious moments, but love-sick and ridiculous – Zeus transformed into a bull for love, and Hera green with jealousy. But, far more unforgivable than this, the work was perfect. Arachne's tapestry was in every way the equal of Athene's.

The goddess saw this at a glance. With one hand she gripped the tapestry at the top of its frame and ripped the cloth from top to bottom.

'Arachne must begin her work again,' she hissed, 'and again, and again. Hateful girl, you shall weave for ever, and nobody will want your tapestries upon their walls.' With her shuttle the goddess struck Arachne on the forehead. At once the girl began to shrink. She grew smaller and smaller, her slim body became round and bloated and her limbs vanished, leaving only the fingers of which she had been so proud, which now sprouted from her shoulders in the form of quivering black legs.

Her friends and admirers shrieked in horror and dismay, jumping back from the shrivelled form upon the floor. For Arachne had become a spider which scuttled to hide in a cranny. Not until night did she venture to crawl out and spin her web across a corner of the loom. And from that day Arachne and her descendants have been spinning, and people say, 'There's another cobweb,' and brush their work away.

ECHO AND NARCISSUS

Hera, the queen of the gods, was stately, beautiful and quick-tempered. Zeus had loved her deeply when he married her, and did so still in his own fashion. Those who showed lack of admiration or respect for her soon felt his anger. But very often he preferred the company of sweeter-natured beauties. The wood nymphs were among his favourites.

When Hera suspected some new rival reigned she would appear among the wood nymphs and question them closely to ferret out the truth. It was difficult to face Hera's penetrating gaze and not to stammer and say something stupid when Zeus was hiding in the trees nearby. Hera was approaching the woods one day when the nymph Echo came running out to meet her. She was the greatest gossip of them all. The Queen of Olympus stood listening for at least half an hour to various stories of what so-and-so had said or done. She believed that she was learning forest secrets from the nymph. Her fury was indescribable when she found that Echo had kept her listening to allow Zeus to make his exit. 'Echo enjoys repeating the words of others,' she said venomously. 'In future those shall be her only speech. She shall say nothing else.'

'Nothing else?' asked Echo, trembling at the goddess's glance. From that moment she could only repeat the last few words she heard. Unable any longer to chatter, she took to wandering by herself in the forest. One day she noticed a young huntsman striding through the trees. She thought he looked more beautiful than the gods and fell hopelessly in love with him. She lay in wait for him daily and followed him through the forest, trying with pleading eyes and outstretched arms to tell him she adored him. The young man, whose name was Narcissus, was used to adoration. Countless wood nymphs had loved him in vain. He thought love a waste of time and jeered at them cruelly. Echo's devotion infuriated him. 'Do you think

I want to see you all the time?' he shouted angrily at her.

'I want to see you all the time!' replied Echo, delighted with this gift of words. This made Narcissus crosser still.

The wood nymphs decided that Narcissus's cruelty had gone too far. All those who had once loved him made a plan. They went to Nemesis, of all the goddesses the one that men most fear. It is she who humbles the proud and punishes the wicked. They begged her for vengeance on Narcissus. 'Make him fall in love more hopelessly than we have done' they prayed.

Nemesis smiled with cruel pleasure. 'He shall love no one but himself,' she said.

There was a clearing in the forest where branches were reflected in the water of a clear still pool. Narcissus went there in the heat of the day and lay down to rest near the water's edge. He saw his face reflected in the pool and was struck by its beauty. He was studying it when Echo came stealing up behind him. She wrapped her arms around his neck and kissed his cheek. 'Get away' said Narcissus, shaking her off, his beautiful face distorted and ugly with rage. 'I don't love you and I never will. I never want to hear your voice or look into your face again.'

'Look into your face again, again, again, again,' sobbed Echo.

'Look into my face,' mocked Narcissus, who enjoyed turning Echo's helpless words against her. 'Now that makes sense. The only thing I've ever heard you say that does.' He moved his head to the right to admire his

profile, and then to the left. He sighed with satisfaction. 'You are flawless: beautiful as the day,' he told the reflection smiling in the water.

Echo fled further into the mountains and hid herself in a cave. Grief made her so ill that she could neither eat nor sleep. Her youthful face grew sharp and withered; daily she became thinner until she wasted to nothing but living bones. Hera at last took pity on her and turned her bones to rock, so that Echo rested at last among the mountains. Nothing was left of her but a thin sad voice, which still haunts caverns and lonely mountain places, waiting to answer you if you call.

Narcissus never noticed she had left him. He lay by the water's edge all day gazing into the pool, entranced. Narcissus, who had despised the love of women, now doted on a face in the water. He leaned to kiss its beautiful forehead but it vanished as his lips touched the water. 'Come back to me,' he begged and as the ripples stilled, the face he longed for reappeared. At night he could not tear himself away. His friends came every

day looking for him but could make no sense of what he said. 'Why does it give me hope, then mock me? I know it loves me for it smiles at me and comes to meet me when I stoop to it.' No one could persuade him to leave the forest pool. Day after day he lay, peering distractedly into the water, until hopeless love wasted his strength away entirely and he died.

The nymphs who had loved him were then truly sorry that they had brought about his death. 'Narcissus, farewell' they lamented. 'Farewell…farewell…farewell…' repeated Echo. When the nymphs came with funeral torches to bear away his body, they found nothing by the pool. In his place a yellow flower was growing. They had never seen one like it before. It stood among the soft grass at the water's edge, tossing its head in the wind, turning to this side and to that, and nodding whenever the breeze fell, as though it were gazing in the water. The nymphs named the flower Narcissus. We know it well today, for Narcissus is the Greek name for the daffodil.

DAPHNE AND APOLLO

In the warm Mediterranean lands there grows a wild evergreen with aromatic leaves, known as the bay tree. In ancient Greece the bay was sacred to Apollo, god of music and poetry, the most famous of the sons of Zeus. The bay was his first love, a love he never forgot, wearing a garland of bay leaves in its memory. But why should a god love a tree? It came about like this.

One day Apollo was feeling particularly pleased. He was then still a young, untried god and had performed his first glorious deed. He had slain a horrifying monster called the Python, a serpent whose poisonous body had covered an entire hillside. He had needed a thousand arrows to kill it. Later he became known as the god of archery – besides being a musician and poet, a god of healing, and one who foretold the future.

In this cheerful mood, Apollo was strolling down the slopes of Mount Parnassus, a favourite haunt of the gods, when he saw Eros, the young son of beautiful Aphrodite, the goddess of love. Eros was practising with a bow and arrows, his face all concentration. Apollo, who considered Eros just a boy, said smiling, 'I wouldn't like to be a Python who met you round a corner.' Eros flushed with anger; he knew Apollo was making fun of him. He was even more furious when Apollo pinched his arm and added, 'You need real muscle for archery. And those darts of yours will only make a scratch.' The look in Eros's eyes was so venomous that Apollo pulled his hair to show that it was all a joke and went off down the hill.

Eros, already almost full-grown, hated to be treated like a child. He had a face as beautiful as his mother's and a pair of silver-feathered wings which carried him through the air on Aphrodite's errands. Mother and son could both wound people's hearts, and Apollo would have been wise to remember this before making fun of Eros. But Apollo had never been in

love, so he never gave the matter a thought.

Eros spread his wings – they were wide and strong, more like an eagle's than a dove's – and flew to the peak of Mount Parnassus, to ponder revenge. In the wooded slopes below he thought he caught a glimpse of the nymph Daphne running through the trees. Yes, it was Daphne, intent on one of her wild schemes – catching a hare, perhaps, and training it to follow her, or racing with deer. Eros grinned, for he had made his plan.

Daphne was the shy daughter of a kind old river god called Peneus and she was a great worry to him. As a child she had been unlike other nymphs; she was only happy playing by herself. When she grew up, men did not interest her. This perplexed her father. He thought his daughter should marry and many men admired her, but when he spoke of choosing a husband for her she had begged him not to. 'I don't want to marry, Father. I want to be outdoors and free. Promise me I need never belong to any man.' So, unwillingly, Peneus had promised, for he loved his daughter dearly.

Eros watched and waited till Apollo, smiling, handsome, and self-satisfied, came to the stretch of wood where Daphne wandered. From among the arrows that Apollo had mocked, Eros chose two: one golden and sharp tipped, the other dull and tipped with lead. Though Eros's darts never killed they were very damaging. Any man or woman struck by a golden arrow fell in love with the first person they saw. The leaden arrows made them hate. Eros took

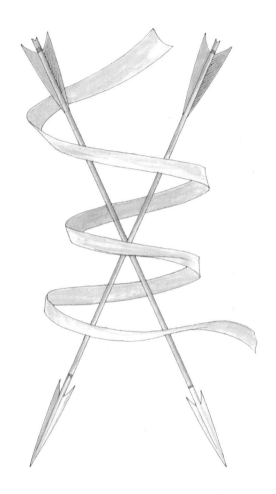

meadows and through the woods, not minding that brambles tore her legs and sharp stones cut her feet; her hair streamed behind her. Apollo's love grew stronger every moment. He could not believe this wild girl did not want his love. He called out, gasping as he ran, 'Daughter of Peneus, do not torment me. All that I have is yours. My poetry and my lyre shall praise you, my healing arts shall serve you. Alas, that I who know the secrets of all herbs and can foretell the future could not foresee this love and know no herb to cure it.'

Though Daphne ran like the wind Apollo ran faster and was gaining on her. She seemed to feel his breath and dreaded his touch. Her strength was failing and Apollo's arms were almost round her when she reached the rocky banks of the river Peneus, and called in desperation to her father, 'Father, remember your promise. Save me!'

Beneath the waters Peneus heard his daughter. Her feet were caught by the rocks of the river bank and held firm. She flung up her arms in despair and found her fingers sprouting leaves; her limbs grew stiff; her panting ceased and her fear began to ebb away. When Apollo's arms encircled her he found he was clasping the smooth bark of a tree. The god grieved bitterly to think his eagerness had robbed him of his love. Daphne had become a bay tree by the river, for ever close to her father. 'Her leaves shall be forever green,' vowed Apollo, 'and I will wear them always and hang my lyre on her branches.'

aim and struck Apollo with the golden arrow. Immediately Apollo, seeing Daphne, was entranced by her wild beauty and tried to talk to her. But the leaden arrow had chilled Daphne's heart. She shuddered at the sight of the god and hurried on. Apollo blamed himself for frightening her. 'Forgive me,' he called. 'I mean no harm. I love you, more than all the world.' Then seeing her disappearing through the trees he hastened after her, beseeching her to stop. 'Daphne, Daphne, am I a monster? It is I, Apollo. No one could love you better.' But the more he pleaded the faster Daphne fled. She ran across the

EROS AND PSYCHE

Psyche and her two sisters were the loveliest girls in Greece. The elder sisters were vain but Psyche, the loveliest, never thought of her beauty. People threw flowers before her and called her the queen of love.

This title properly belonged to Aphrodite. When the goddess heard that people threw garlands before a mere girl, she grew angry. 'How dare they make offerings to a mortal? I'll see this beauty for myself.' One glance was enough. The goddess was ravaged with envy and jealousy. It was no comfort to remind herself that mortal beauty withers. Aphrodite vowed to make Psyche suffer.

From that moment Psyche's perfection cast a chill on people's hearts. Though all men sang her praises none loved her. Her sisters married and still no suitors came for Psyche. Her despairing parents consulted Apollo's oracle at Delphi. 'A husband waits for your daughter. He is feared by men and gods alike,' the oracle declared. 'Leave Psyche on the mountain top and he will fetch her.'

So the wedding procession with bridal torches wound up the mountainside and left Psyche on the bare summit, alone and shivering. Clouds swirled around her feet and a strong wind blew. 'Do not fear, Psyche,' the wind said. 'Leap from the precipice and I will catch you.' Psyche was terrified but the voice seemed to be her friend so she stepped into the air. She felt herself caught and lifted up and the air roared in her ears. Then the wind grew soft and gentle. Down, down, she came and was laid in soft meadow-grass, where she fell asleep.

She awoke in a scented garden in the middle of which was a palace. The servants were expecting her. Their master, they said, would return at nightfall. Psyche went to the chamber prepared for her and waited. When it was dark her husband came and took her in his arms. 'I have been

watching and waiting,' he said. 'I was afraid you would not come.' Psyche felt safe and happy. But before it grew light he left her, promising to return at nightfall. So the days slipped by. Psyche spent every night with her husband but he always left before it was light enough to see him. At last she begged to see his face.

'You must not ask that,' he replied. 'If you saw my face or knew my name, we would have to part. Trust me and all will be well'.

Psyche had to be content with this. She lived so happily in the enchanted palace that she forgot for many weeks that her parents and sisters had no idea what had become of her. Then she begged to be allowed to tell them of her happiness. The wind lifted her in its arms and brought her to her parents who were overjoyed to see her. She told them that she lived in a palace and had the kindest husband in the world.

'Who is he? What does he look like?' asked her sisters.

Psyche had to confess that she had never seen him. Her sisters were envious of her palace and fine garden. They told her they thought her husband must be hideous, a monster, a serpent putting on a sweet voice to deceive her. 'He will eat you when he's tired of you,' they said.

Psyche became so miserable that she was glad when the time came to leave. Her sisters' words echoed in her head. When her husband was asleep she fetched an oil lamp and, shielding the little flame with her hand, tiptoed to the bed. It was no monster, but

Aphrodite's son Eros, the god of love himself, matchlessly beautiful. As Psyche stood gazing, the lamp tilted and spilt scalding oil on Eros's shoulder. He awoke and saw her. 'Psyche!' he cried. 'Why did you not trust me? Love and suspicion cannot live together.' And he spread his wings and was gone.

Psyche sobbed herself to sleep. She awoke to find herself at the gate of her old home. When her family learned of the husband she had lost, her sisters were secretly delighted. Each thought, 'Eros may like me better.' Without telling the other, each made her way up the mountain and called to the wind Psyche had described, and leapt into the air. But the wind did not answer the sisters' calls and they were dashed to pieces on the rocks.

Psyche waited and hoped, but Eros did not return. So she decided to search for him. She journeyed through towns and countryside and met many people who had felt Eros's arrows but none knew where he lived. She rested in a temple of Demeter and the goddess gave her good advice. 'Go to Aphrodite and beg her to forgive you. She is unreasonable, but you must try. Eros tried to keep your marriage secret for fear of what his mother might do. Without her goodwill you will never find him.'

Psyche went trembling to Aphrodite's temple and bowed before the altar. The goddess was delighted to see her rival looking so pale and careworn. She set her to work. She took Psyche to a barn where she kept food for her doves. It was full of grain

in heaps: wheat, rye, barley and millet, all mixed together. 'It needs sorting,' said Aphrodite. 'Separate it into piles, one of each kind of grain, and do it by this evening.'

So Psyche began, but after an hour she had not sorted more than a cupful. She was sitting in despair on the floor of the barn when she saw a colony of ants marching across it. They went directly to the grain. To and fro, never stopping, each ant carried a grain from one heap to another until, by darkness, all was sorted.

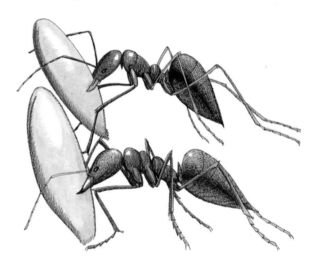

Aphrodite was furious. 'Someone's been helping you! You won't win my respect by cheating.' She tossed Psyche some black bread to eat and left her.

The following day the goddess said, 'Cross the river and bring me wool from the golden sheep that graze on the other bank.' Psyche was wading across when she heard the reeds whispering, 'Take care, Psyche. The rams are savage. They will rip you to pieces if you cross now. Wait until the midday heat makes the flock drowsy. Then collect the wool that clings to the brambles.' Psyche did as the reeds advised and brought Aphrodite an armful of golden wool.

Aphrodite grew angrier than ever. 'Go to the land of the dead,' she ordered. 'Ask Persephone to put a little of her beauty in this casket. I need it to repair the damage my son's treachery has done to mine.' Psyche thought of killing herself as the only means she knew of reaching the land of the dead. But a voice whispered, 'Psyche, do not be so rash. That way you will never return.' The voice told her how to find the cave that led to the underworld, how to cross the River Styx that encircled it and how to pass Cerberus, the three-headed dog that barred the way. 'But do not look inside the casket,' the voice warned. Psyche followed its guidance faithfully, was received kindly by Persephone and hastened with the filled casket back to the daylight. Then a cruel thought struck her. 'With all my misfortunes I will have grown sad and ugly.' So she opened the casket to take a tiny scrap of beauty. But the box contained the sleep of death, and she fell senseless to the ground.

Eros, who had been protecting Psyche, sped to Olympus. 'Take pity on us, Zeus,' he entreated. Zeus sent Hermes down to shake Psyche from her sleep and bring her to Mount Olympus. On Olympus Zeus offered her ambrosia, the drink of the gods. 'Drink it and be immortal,' he said. So death's sleep lost its power over Psyche and she was united with Eros for ever. But it was a long time before Aphrodite forgave them.

THE STORY OF CADMUS

King Agenor of Tyre had three sons and a lovely daughter called Europa. One day as Europa walked on the sea-shore with her friends she saw that her father's cattle had left their pastures and were wandering on the sand. There was a fine, large, snow-white bull among them. Its short, neat horns shone as though a jeweller had been polishing their ivory. Europa thought it odd that she had never noticed such a handsome beast before. The bull came up to her and nuzzled her hand. She offered it flowers to eat, and made a garland for its horns. It seemed as gentle as a lamb, so she climbed upon its back and let it amble with her to the edge of the sea.

'Where are you off to?' laughed her friends. But they stopped laughing when the bull lunged forward, plunged into the water and swam powerfully out to sea, with Europa clinging to its horns and calling for help. Some of her friends ran to the king, while others stared after the bull which soon became a faraway speck on the water – and then was out of sight.

King Agenor was beside himself with grief, for Europa was his favourite child. He was in a great rage too, because he did not know whom to blame and there was no one he could punish. He called his three sons to him and said, 'Go and find your sister. Search every corner of the world for her and do not come back to my kingdom without her.'

The three young men set sail at once. They had no idea which way the bull had gone, so each steered a different course. The eldest son sailed to the west, and reached a pleasant coast where he founded a kingdom and thought no more about Europa. The second son sailed north until he came to an island where the hills were full of gold. There he stopped to make his fortune and quite forgot his sister. The youngest son, whose name was Cadmus, went north, south, east and west, searching the whole world to find her. His journeying took him to Greece, where he asked everyone for news of his sister, but people shook their heads and seemed to think his errand was a hopeless one. Yet he would not give up. 'I will ask Apollo to tell me where she is' he decided.

Apollo, who saw the future, had an oracle at Delphi where his priestess uttered the words he breathed into her body. Cadmus entered the temple and put his question to the god's interpreter. The oracle's answers were often more like riddles than replies to questions, but to Cadmus Apollo spoke plainly enough: 'Abandon your search for your sister. You will never find her. The bull that bore her off was Zeus himself who has taken her to be his bride. Look instead for a young cow that has no master and has never been yoked to a plough. Follow wherever she leads, and where she lies down to rest, there you must build a city, and you shall be its king.'

Cadmus went away perplexed and sad. He must give up his sister, for no one can claim back what the gods have stolen, but he was tired of wandering, and how, among all the cattle of the world, was he to find the one that he should follow? But almost at once he saw on the road ahead of him a young heifer walking slowly along, with no one to guide her. He tried to catch her up to see if her neck bore any mark of a harness but she quickened her pace, and at whatever speed he went he found the cow was always just ahead of him. He saw that on each flank she had a round white patch, like the moon. 'This is Apollo's sign,' he thought, and thanked

the god in his heart. The heifer was tireless. She went over mountains and through forest without resting. At night she stood with closed eyes while Cadmus stretched out exhausted beside her. After many days she brought him to a hill that overlooked a grassy plain, and here she sank to her knees and lay down in the grass.

'The gods have chosen – this shall be my home,' said Cadmus.' But how shall I build a city with no hands but my own?' He looked around. Plenty of trees for timber, he thought, and the sound of running water. The water came from a spring that bubbled from a low cave in the midst of a tangled thicket. Cadmus was thirsty and fought his way in, for there was no path. As he bent to drink, a huge serpent slid out of the black mouth of the cave and reared its head over him. Its breath was fire, for it was a dragon. Cadmus seized his spear and drove it deep into the monster's throat. The dragon writhed and reared and lashed at him with its tail. Cadmus clung to his spear and the creature shook him to and fro. As they battled amongst the trees he trapped its head against a trunk and leaned on his spear with all his weight. The tip went through the dragon's skull and killed the brute.

Cadmus was still panting with the effort when a clear voice behind him said, 'Cadmus, well done, but there is more still to do.'

He turned and saw the tall figure and grave face of the goddess Athene who stood among the trees, dressed in gleaming gold armour. 'I have been watching over your wanderings,' she said, 'for you are to be the

ruler of a great city - if you obey me now. While the blood of the dragon is still hot, draw out its teeth and sow them in the field where the heifer rests. And when the crop grows, throw a stone into the midst of it.'

Cadmus did as Athene commanded. He scattered the teeth like seed over the field. At once the ground heaved and split and spears thrust up through the soil. Helmeted heads, shoulders and breast-plates appeared. All over the field the teeth sprouted men in armour. As soon as their arms were free they brandished their swords. They sprang from the soil, a menacing army looking for an enemy. Cadmus seized a stone and hurled it into the midst of them.

'You struck me, brother!' cried one man to his neighbour, and dealt him a savage blow. The attacked man struck back, but hit a third. The quarrel spread until the whole field was fighting. The battle raged until the ground was deep in corpses and only five men remained alive. These successful warriors came to Cadmus and offered to serve him.

With these five followers Cadmus built Thebes, the famous city of a hundred gates. This so pleased Athene that she gave Cadmus a goddess as his bride - Harmonia, daughter of Aphrodite and Ares god of war. For this great marriage, the first between a goddess and a mortal, all the gods came down from Olympus, bearing gifts. Among these was a magnificent robe and a necklace which were to play an ominous part in the story of the city - but that is another tale.

MELEAGER AND THE BLAZING LOG

Oeneus, king of Calydon, and his queen, Althaea, had daughters but no heir. When at last the queen gave birth to a son there was rejoicing throughout the land. The newborn child was wrapped up snugly and put in a cot beside its mother's bed. Many times in the night Althaea leant over and looked into the sleeping baby's face. She thought that no young prince, no baby in the world could have looked more beautiful. She was sinking back to rest again when she saw figures in the room. 'The door did not open,' she thought. Yet three women, their faces hidden in grey cloaks, were seated by the fire. Althaea knew then that they were the three terrible sisters, the Fates, who spin the thread of destiny for each of us.

'This child will be strong and handsome,' said the first sister, drawing the raw wool from her distaff and twisting it with withered fingers.

'He will be bold,' said the second, drawing out the thread. 'Let no man say him nay.'

The third sister drew a pair of scissors from her cloak. 'He will live no longer than that log shall last upon the fire,' she said and went to cut the thread. Instantly Althaea leapt from her bed, thrust her hand into the fire and drew out the blazing log. She beat it frantically on the floor to knock the glowing charcoal from its end. Then she wrapped the blackened stump carefully in a cloth and locked it in a chest. The dawn light came; the Fates were gone; the baby slept peacefully. The parents named the boy Meleager.

Meleager grew up to be as fine a prince as the Fates had predicted. He was brave, even reckless, and loved to be out of doors racing, wrestling and hunting. He was vexed that his father's kingdom lacked any enemy for him to pursue. But the peace which he found so tedious was fated not to last. King Oeneus had the ill-luck to offend Artemis, the huntress goddess.

Without meaning any disrespect he quite forgot to honour her among the gods to whom he sacrificed at harvest time. Nothing enraged the immortals more than a suspected insult. When offerings were made in Calydon to Demeter, to Dionysus and to Athene, and Artemis found her altar bare, the furious goddess sent a boar to devastate the land, a huge brute, larger than a bull. Its neck was high-arched and bristled with a crest that stood along its spine like a row of spears. It spewed hot foam; its tusks were like the elephant's; its breath scorched roots and branches. The whole kingdom was torn and trampled by it. The beast turned forests to a cinder, flattened corn and ripped grapes from the vines. It gored cattle and killed the shepherds. Villagers threw their belongings into carts and fled to the city.

Oeneus sent heralds far and near, promising a great boar hunt, to rid him of the boar. Whoever killed the boar should keep its pelt and tusks. From all over Greece men eager for glory arrived for the hunt. Theseus, Peleus and Jason came, and many others, including Meleager's two uncles, the brothers of Althaea. A tall, fair stranger arrived, carrying a bow and ivory quiver; he lifted his travelling hat and shook loose a heavy knot of hair, proving to everyone's amazement to be a woman. Her name was Atalanta.

King Oeneus entertained the hunters for nine days and nights. Artemis heard their shouts and laughter and, knowing what they were about, soured their tempers. Some grumbled that a hunting party was no place

for a woman. Meleager's uncles had taken a particular dislike to Atalanta. 'Have we been brought here to play women's games?' said one to the other.

Meleager flushed crimson and shouted, 'There is no hunter here whose skill I question.' Men exchanged glances and smiled, for it was plain that Meleager was in love with the beautiful stranger, though she ignored him.

With ill-feeling in their hearts the hunters set off on the tenth day, some armed with bows and arrows, others with boar-spears, javelins or axes, all anxious to be the one to strike the death blow. The boar was discovered lurking in some willows. It bounded out, killing two huntsmen and sending others scrambling for safety. Atalanta let fly an arrow which halted it a moment, but it charged again and disembowelled a hunter. Then weapons were hurled in a frenzy, until Meleager's javelin pierced the

beast's flank and as it whirled around in pain he drove his hunting spear deep under its shoulderblade to the heart.

Meleager had killed the boar and won its pelt and tusks. But when the animal was skinned he presented the coveted trophies to Atalanta. 'Your arrow struck first,' he said. 'If we had left the beast alone you would have killed it.' At once an argument broke out. It was against the rules of courtesy to give away the trophy to anybody but the person of highest rank. This was Meleager's elder uncle, brother-in-law to the king. Furious at the insult, he seized the pelt from Atalanta. Meleager struck him in a rage. His brother joined the fray; knives were drawn and Meleager killed his uncles.

Althaea saw the two corpses carried in a sad procession through the city gates. She recognized her brothers and was told they had been murdered. She raised her hands to heaven. 'Who is their murderer?' she demanded. 'By the gods I swear I shall not rest until I see him dead.'

'It is your son,' they said.

Not pausing to allow herself one instant's thought, Althaea ran to the chest, seized the blackened log and threw it upon the fire. She watched it burn until it was a heap of ashes.

Meleager, returning from the hunt, was seized with pains like fire, fell to the ground, and was carried home dead by his companions. His mother destroyed herself for grief and his sisters wept ceaselessly, so that Artemis relented and in pity for them changed them into birds.

ATALANTA AND THE GOLDEN APPLES

There is more to tell of Atalanta, the mysterious huntress who was the cause of such disaster in Calydon. She was the daughter of Iasus, a prince of Argos, who had longed for a son for many years. When Atalanta was born he was so disappointed that he ordered the child to be left on a hillside to die. Artemis, the wild huntress-goddess, found the sleeping baby and sent a she-bear to look after it. A band of woodlanders saw the bear suckling her cubs in the mouth of her cave with a human child snuggled amongst them. Too wise to rob the bear directly of her young, they waited until they found the cubs untended and took the child away to be cared for properly.

So Atalanta was brought up in the wilds among simple country people, which suited her better than a palace. The bear's milk had made her so strong and forceful that despite her beauty she was treated as a boy. She handled weapons and hunted with the men, who thought of her as an equal. None of them would have dared to talk to her of love, for Atalanta despised softness and love never entered her head.

Atalanta's attitude delighted Artemis, who detested love and punished any who dared to admire her moonlit beauty. She wanted Atalanta to join the huntress nymphs who were her followers, and gave her a grave warning: 'Never marry, for if you marry you will become a captive till the end of your days.'

When Iasus heard of the golden-haired huntress who had appeared out of the wilds and shown such skill and courage in the boar hunt, he sent messengers to discover the truth about the girl. Then father and daughter were reconciled. Iasus was overjoyed; no son could have made him feel prouder. Nevertheless he felt his daughter should now behave as other daughters did. Almost his first words to her were, 'Now we must

find a husband for you.' Atalanta hated the idea and would not hear of it. In the end she said, 'Father, I agree on one condition. The man who marries me must have outrun me in a race. If any man wishes to try, and I outrun him, I shall kill him with my arrow.' Many suitors were eager for the hand of Atalanta. They made light of the sinister condition, for it should not be difficult to outrun a girl. Then they learned their mistake, for Atalanta ran faster than the wind and though each suitor went smiling to the starting point of the race, none reached the winning post ahead of her. Atalanta made each one pay the penalty.

Even when it was known that to race Atalanta meant certain death there were many men so in love with her that they were willing to try. 'What fools they are,' exclaimed a young man called Hippomenes when he heard of these infatuated suitors racing to their death. 'I wouldn't risk my life for a woman.' But the more Hippomenes thought about it the more curious he became to see this woman who could rob men of every shred of common sense. When the next hopeful suitors came along Hippomenes was among the crowd that watched them race. When he saw Atalanta dart forward he felt as though her arrow had already pierced his heart. Her beauty was so dazzling that it pained him to look at her. 'Now I understand' he said, and hoped savagely that none of these young men would live to marry her. For Hippomenes had decided that at all costs he would run the race.

Knowing how foolish it would be to rely on his skill as a runner - though Atalanta gave all her suitors a head start - Hippomenes prayed to Aphrodite for help. The goddess of love was by no means pleased with Atalanta's attitude and very willingly listened to him. She gave him three golden apples from the tree that grew before her temple. 'Use these as I tell you,' she said, 'and you will win the race.'

Hippomenes begged Iasus to let him be the next to run. When Atalanta saw his eager, handsome face she felt such a liking for him that she hesitated.

'The crowd is waiting' said her father, 'will you run or not?'

Then Atalanta brushed these foolish feelings aside. She sprang from the starting post and was soon level with Hippomenes, despite his start. As he ran he took one of the golden apples and bowled it fast along the ground, across her path. Atalanta saw it gleam and paused to pick it up. In that instant Hippomenes shot past, straining every muscle to keep ahead. He had not reached the half-way mark when Atalanta overtook him. Hippomenes rolled the second apple in her way. Again, though she could not have said why, she felt she must have it. As she ran aside to get it Hippomenes passed her again. He was in sight of the the winning post when she sped by him, and in desperation he threw the last apple. Despite herself Atalanta stopped. Aphrodite's fruit seemed to beckon and she must have it. As she stretched her hand to it she heard the crowd cheering. Hippomenes had won the race and she was his.

So Atalanta was married to a husband whom she liked better than any other man. Hippomenes was totally wrapped up in his new happiness, and never gave a thought to Aphrodite who had brought it all about. Such neglect of the gods is dangerous. The goddess angrily waited for offerings to be placed upon her altar, or songs sung to her or poems recited in her praise. When none appeared she stepped into her swan-drawn chariot and flew to consult Rhea, the mother of the gods, about a suitable punishment. Rhea turned Atalanta and Hippomenes into lions and harnessed them to her chariot, which ever afterwards they had to drag. So Atalanta became a captive all her days.

JASON AND THE GOLDEN FLEECE

Aeson, king of Iolcos in Thessaly, had a treacherous brother called Pelias. Guileless Aeson was no match for Pelias, who seized his throne and drove him into exile. Aeson took away with him his little son Jason, thinking, 'I must hide the child or his uncle will kill him, because he is the true heir.' He gave Jason to Chiron, the wisest of the centaurs, creatures who are men to the waist but have the body of a horse. So Jason spent his childhood in Chiron's cave on Mount Pelion, and the learned and kindly centaur taught him to be brave, self-reliant and just.

Chiron could see into the future. One day he called Jason and said, 'You are now a man and will do much. There are many dangers in your path. Never take the easier way unless it is the better way and you will deserve the goodwill of the gods.' Then he gave Jason a leopard-skin cloak and two broad-bladed spears and sent him into the world.

Jason had a clear idea where he was going. Many times he had looked out across the plain to Iolcos. This land was rightfully his kingdom and he meant to claim it. As he journeyed he came to a river swirling in full flood. An old woman sat by the bank moaning, 'Who will carry me across?' To Jason the river looked dangerous to cross even without a burden and he was about to ignore her. Then he thought of Chiron's words and offered his help. The old woman leapt on his back as nimbly as a goat and proved amazingly heavy. Jason staggered in the water and lost a shoe in midstream, but he got over somehow and set her down. Then she grew straight and shining, like a pillar of light, and said, 'I am Hera, wife of Zeus and Queen of Olympus. As you have helped me, so I will help you when you are in need.' Jason flung himself to the ground before the goddess. When he lifted his head she was gone.

Jason strode on into Iolcos. He asked for an audience with the king,

whose eyes darted uneasily over his long wild hair, leopard skin and unshod foot. It had been foretold that a man without a shoe would take Pelias' kingdom from him. Pelias hid his fear and asked the stranger who he was. Jason revealed himself courteously to his uncle and proposed an agreement. Pelias should keep the wealth and lands but surrender the kingship to Jason.

Pelias seemed ready to agree. 'I am old and need someone to lift the cares of governing from my shoulders,' he said. 'But to be sure that you are worthy I will ask you to do me a service. You have heard of the Golden Fleece that hangs on a sacred oak tree in the land of King Aeetes of Colchis. That fleece belongs by rights to us. The ghost of our kinsman Phrixus cannot rest, nor can Iolcos thrive, until the golden fleece is brought back here. Fetch it and you shall have the kingdom.'

Jason could not refuse, though the tale of the ghost was an invention to get rid of him. For Colchis was a land at the edge of the world. All manner of perils beset the route and the fleece was guarded by an immortal serpent sacred to Ares, the god of war. To get there Jason needed an extraordinarily fast ship and brave companions. He sent heralds to invite the bravest heroes in Greece to join his expedition. On the seashore he ordered the best boatbuilder in Greece to make him a magnificent ship. No one had seen the like of it before – for until then no boat in the world had attempted to voyage so far upon the open seas. The ship was named the Argo, which means swift, for she had two mighty sails and space for fifty oarsmen. Fifty heroes answered Jason's call and they manned the oars as the Argo was launched to sail for Colchis.

The Argonauts, as Jason and his crew were called, needed enormous strength and courage to escape the snares and outwit the enemies they met upon their voyage. After many perils, too many to tell here, the exhausted Argonauts put ashore to the court of King Phineus in Thrace. He looked haggard and despairing, for his palace was at the mercy of a pair of Harpies – loathsome winged creatures with women's heads – who at every meal flew in and snatched food from the table, spattering their droppings on the rest so that it stank and was not fit to eat. Jason and his crew so minced the Harpies with their sharp swords that they fled out to sea and never troubled Phineus again.

Afloat again, the Argonauts were tossed day and night on a black, boiling sea until at last they reached Colchis, a land so remote that its gods were strange and hostile, and its people dealt in magic. The Argonauts decided that Jason should first go to King Aeetes and ask for the fleece as a favour. If it were refused the Argonauts would go to war.

King Aeetes was enraged. 'Return the way you have come,' he cried, 'before I have your tongues cut out and your hands lopped off.' But his raven-haired daughter, Medea, who was a sorceress, calmed him with fair words. Jason could have the fleece, the king then said, if he could yoke two fire-breathing, brazen-footed bulls and plough a field with them, and sow it with dragon's teeth. This he must do in one day. Jason was wondering how he could ever manage these tasks when Medea came to him, offering help in return for marriage. For the sorceress was in love with him. Hera, remembering her promise, had touched Medea's heart. Medea gave Jason a blood-red lotion to bathe his body, his spear and his shield, so that the bulls' breath could not scorch them, and told him that when he had sown the teeth he must throw a stone in the midst of the field. Jason yoked the terrible bulls, ploughed all day, and at nightfall sowed the teeth, from which armed men sprang up - for these were seeds left over from Cadmus's sowing at Thebes - and as before the stone set them quarrelling and they destroyed each other.

Then King Aeetes, who had never meant to part with the fleece, refused to hand it over. He planned instead to burn Jason's boat and murder all the crew. But Medea learned of this and went to Jason in the night. She led him in the moonlight to the ghostly thicket of trees where the golden fleece glittered on the sacred oak. The tree was wrapped in the thousand coils of an enormous serpent, which it was pointless to attack for it was born from the blood of the Titans and was immortal. Medea soothed it with spells and sprinkled sleep in its eyes. Jason stealthily unfastened the fleece and together he and Medea fled to the beach where the Argo lay.

The Argonauts were on the open sea when the dawn light showed Aeetes' ships following fast in pursuit. Medea seized hold of her young half-brother, Apsyrtus, whom she had brought with her. 'Kill him,' she said 'and cut him into pieces!' Then she threw the pieces one by one into the sea. While her father stopped to collect his son's body piece by piece from the waters to give him a proper burial, the Argo sped back to Colchis.

Jason and his dark-eyed bride were received by the people with joy and the fleece was hung in the temple of Zeus. Jason was declared king of Colchis, for he forced Pelias to keep his word. But Medea loved revenge, and did not mean to let the old tyrant die in peace. She told his daughters, 'I can make the old young again. I'll show you how easy it is.' She took an old ram, and cut it in bits, and put it in a boiling cauldron with magic herbs, uttered a spell, and the ram leapt out - a young lamb again. Then she said to

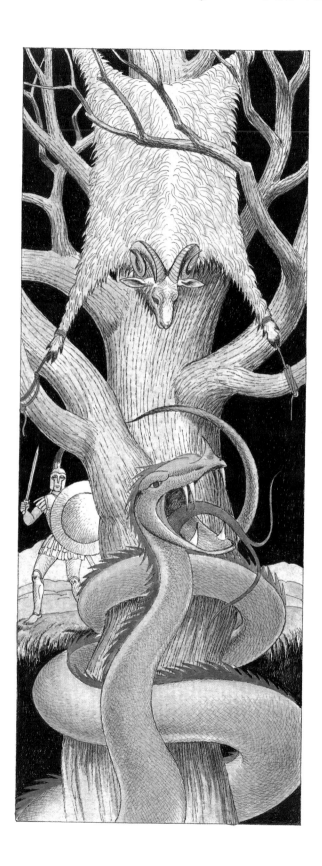

Pelias's daughters, 'Do this to your father and he will be young once more.' But she only told them half the spell. They cut their father in pieces and boiled him, but he never came to life again.

Jason grew to hate Medea for her savage ways and took a kindly wife instead – Glauce, a princess of Corinth. Medea's revenge was terrible. She summoned her two young sons born to Jason and sent them with a wedding gift to Glauce, a golden crown and long white robe, both dipped in poison. When Glauce put them on she was burned as if by fire. When the children returned Medea killed them to prevent Jason having them. Then she rose into the air in a chariot drawn by winged serpents and left him for ever. Many more stories are told about Medea, and it is said that she became immortal, but Jason led a wandering life and met a sad and lonely death.

ORPHEUS AND EURYDICE

A hero excelled in every physical art that made a warrior strong. But the arts of music and poetry, so the ancient Greeks believed, had a more than earthly power. The hero was mightiest who could master these. Orpheus was such a hero, one of the fearless band who went with Jason to fetch the Golden Fleece. Through the power of music he made the rulers of the dead obey him – or very nearly so. It happened like this.

Orpheus was a mortal, the son of a Thracian king, but his music was godlike. The gods would have been envious had they not been so enchanted. Even Apollo, who had shown mortals how to make music, was happy for his lyre to remain silent while Orpheus sang to his. The animals of the woods and fields came to listen. Birds flew down from the sky – the eagle and the lark together. When he sat in the sun the trees would gather round to listen and he would find himself sitting in leafy shade. The mountains wrinkled their tree-lined foreheads and bent their heads to listen, and when he walked they tried to follow him.

Among the wood nymphs was one who listened more intently than any of the others. Her name was Eurydice. Orpheus sang as if to her alone. He loved her and had set his heart on marrying her, and she loved him. But Hymen, the yellow-robed marriage-god who attends all wedding feasts, brought a sad omen to theirs. The marriage torches he carried would not burn brightly, but smouldered and made the guests' eyes weep.

Not many months after, Eurydice, walking along a river bank, trod on a snake hidden in the grass. It bit her on the ankle and she died.

Orpheus was distraught. He wandered the woods and mountains lamenting. His lyre hung untouched at his side. 'What use is music?' he cried. 'It will not bring Eurydice back.' But after long weeping Orpheus fell to thinking. It seemed a desperate undertaking, but why should he not

go to the underworld and beg its rulers to return Eurydice? He would enchant them with his music. His playing had softened the rocks of the mountains. It would soften the heart of Hades, lord of the dead.

The deep mountain caves that make men shudder lead to Tartarus, the land where the dead dwell as pale shadows of their living selves. But the entrances are few and hard to find. Orpheus, scrambling down one of these, came to the grey banks of the River Styx, whose dull waters encircle the underworld. Charon, the old ferryman who takes the dead across the river, put up a hand to stop him.

But Orpheus took his lyre and played, and even Charon's shrivelled heart could not resist, and he allowed him in.

On the far bank dead shades gathered, wanting to know who brought such magic sounds, and they begged Orpheus to stay and play. The blessed shades that lived in the Elysian Fields had never heard such music. The evil ones, with ceaseless tasks to do, stopped their endless work for one brief moment and listened as he passed. Orpheus entered Hades' dark palace and bowed before the thrones where the lord of the underworld sat with his queen, pale, lovely Persephone, judging the newly dead. They were expecting him, forewarned that a mortal had forced his way into their kingdom with a preposterous request.

Orpheus had no need to think what to say. His words came tumbling out. 'Return Eurydice, I beseech you. I do not wish to steal your subjects - no one would be so

bold. When she is old she will come back to you as all must do. Lend her to me, I beg you, for a few more years...' But while he spoke he saw their faces clouding. Persephone looked sad and shook her head and Hades' cold glance pierced him to the bone.

'No shade returns from Tartarus' he said.

Then Orpheus took his lyre. He plucked its strings and at the first notes Hades closed his eyes to listen. Orpheus sang of love and death, of yearning and unconquerable hope. Very beautiful and strange the music sounded in that still hall. Abruptly, Hades motioned him to stop.

'This is no music for the underworld,' he said. 'The gates of Tartarus would melt before it. Take Eurydice with you and depart.'

Eurydice was summoned from the shadows, pale and wondering. As Orpheus ran to her Hades raised a warning hand.

'She is not yours while she is in my kingdom' he pronounced. 'Turn your back on her and do not look at her until she is in the light of day.'

Orpheus set off with Eurydice following. He sang as he went, to comfort her, but did not turn his head to smile. At Charon's ferry he did not help her in or out. 'Her shade is so light it does not weigh the boat,' he thought, and felt a chill of fear. Was she truly behind him, or was Hades playing a cruel joke? He stopped his song to listen for her footsteps. Yes, he could hear them, following lightly behind. He felt a great wave of relief and happiness. There was not far to go now, but the way was steep and narrow, up hill and very dark. Orpheus climbed steadily, never looking back. He could see the daylight. A few more steps and his dear wife would stand in the warm sun beside him. But, hideous thought, perhaps it was some other long-dead wraith that mocking Hades had sent after him?

He stepped into the sunshine. 'Have you deceived me gods?' he cried, and turned to see.

Eurydice stretched out her longing arms towards him. Unable to climb so swiftly she had not yet reached the daylight. Hades' shadows were still all around her. She faded into the darkness and was gone. So Orpheus lost his beloved wife once more, and this time for ever. He never loved again.

PERSEUS AND THE GORGON'S HEAD

Acrisius, king of Argolis, was a cold-hearted man. His cruelty angered the gods, who decreed he would be killed by his grandson. As the king had only one child, a daughter called Danae, he thought he had made himself safe by imprisoning her in a tower of brass, and letting no man near her.

Danae, wretched and lonely in the tower, grew to be a beautiful woman. Zeus fell in love with her and came to her in the form of a shower of gold, and she bore him a son. When Acrisius learned of this he called a servant and said 'Put Danae and her brat into a chest and throw them into the sea.'

Though the servant was a villain, the sight of Danae shielding her baby in her arms moved him to pity. Instead of hammering down the lid of the chest he sat Danae in it, with the baby in her cloak, and pushed it out to sea. The tide swept the little chest out into the ocean where it bobbed and rolled for a day and a night, Danae feeding the baby at her breast and praying for the tall waves to spare them. On the second day she saw a coast ahead, so set with rocks that she shut her eyes and waited for the sea to smash the chest against them. But a fisherman on the cliff threw his net over the chest and hauled it safely in. When he heard Danae's story he took her to his King, Polydectes, who was lord of this land, the island of Seriphos, and he promised to care for her and her son.

Danae named him Perseus and he grew into a strong, handsome and courageous young man. Polydectes treated them well – too well, for the king paid so much attention to Danae that the whole court remarked on it. Danae, though still beautiful, thought of herself as middle-aged and was astounded when the king declared he must marry her. She did not care for him and told him so. Then Polydectes' kindness evaporated. He was resentful and determined to have his way. He made Danae's life miserable with his threats and coaxing, and Perseus grew angry and protective.

Polydectes planned to get rid of him.

A great festival with sports and banquets was proclaimed. Nobles from throughout the land arrived, and each of them brought the king a gift. Perseus was poor and had nothing to offer and was humiliated when Polydectes made fun of him in front of the guests.

'I may have nothing to give a king but I know how to serve one. Give me a task and I will do it.'

'Then bring me the head of Medusa the Gorgon,' the king replied at once.

Persus saw that he had fallen into a trap, for whoever looked on the face of the Gorgon was turned to stone. But he did not show any concern. 'I will return with it,' he promised.

As he sat later brooding on his task, Athene, the green-eyed goddess of wisdom, came and stood before him. Beside her was Hermes, the messenger of the gods. Athene gave Perseus a shield that shone like a mirror.

'Since you must not look into Medusa's face, look in this mirror instead. Strike at her throat but guide your sword by the reflection.' 'Take my winged sandals for the journey' added Hermes.

'But how shall I know where to find Medusa?' Perseus asked.

'She lives with her two sisters,' replied Athene, 'but to find their lair you must inquire of gods more ancient than I am. In the farthest north, where the sun never shines, is a cave where the Three Grey Sisters sit. Ask them.' Perseus rose high in the air on the winged sandals and sped over land and ocean till he

came to the frozen shore of the furthest coast, where the sand was grey and windswept and the sky was always dark. Hunched on a flat rock before their cave sat the Three Grey Sisters. They were born old and wizened, with only one eye and one tooth to share between them. Perseus found them mumbling over a meal, each chewing in turn. He settled beside them. 'Who's there?' croaked one of them. 'Pass me the eye, sister, and let me look'. As her sister held out the eye, gropingly Perseus took it. He would not return it until the sisters told him how to find Medusa. They cackled and shrieked at him but they were forced to tell. He must go to the Hesperides, the daughters of the Evening Star who live in the Garden of the West. 'They may tell you how to get there, but you won't come back' said the crones, with spite. 'Not without the three gifts, you won't.'

Hermes' winged sandals carried Perseus to the garden where the nymphs danced around a golden-fruited tree. They called to Perseus to join them, and shook their heads sadly when he explained his mission. 'Do not go near Medusa without this cap of darkness to hide you,' they cried, 'and this diamond-bladed sickle to sever her neck, and this goat skin bag to carry away her head.' They gave Perseus the three gifts and pointed the way. He sprang off through the air once more, flying over a plain scattered with strange, contorted rocks, the remains of men and women turned to stone. Perseus put on the cap of darkness, held Athene's shield aloft and turned his head to look in it as he flew. It showed him Medusa and her two sisters basking on the rocks before their cave. Though each was hideous, Medusa was the most terrible, for though she had the body of a woman, she had claws of brass, a neck scaled like a serpent's and, instead of hair, a mass of wriggling serpents that hissed and flicked their tongues continually around her head. Perseus, with eyes fixed on the reflection in the shield, made a clean stroke with the sickle and cut the head from the neck.

Dreadful were the screams of Medusa's sisters. They tore the air with their talons but the invisible enemy had escaped them, soaring into the sky with Medusa's dripping head shrouded in the goatskin bag. Perseus was speeding over the seas now, back to Seriphos. Flying over a rocky coast he noticed a figure far below standing on a pinnacle of rock with waves surging all around. It seemed

to be a statue but, flying closer, he found a living woman chained to the rock. She was too terrified to speak, and Perseus's sudden appearance, when he remembered to take off his cap, increased her fright. He told her he meant no harm, and by gentle questioning learned her story. 'My name is Andromeda, daughter of King Cepheus, the lord of these lands. My mother Cassiopeia loves me so much she boasted that I was more beautiful than the sea nymphs. It made Poseidon so angry that he sent a monster from the bottom of the sea to plague us. It is destroying our kingdom. It floods the land and eats up all the people. I am here as a sacrifice to it, for nothing else will make it go away. An oracle has told my father so.' Perseus was hacking at the iron fetters when the monster's head reared up out of the waves, its jaws open to snatch Andromeda. Perseus swung his diamond sickle and cut off the monster's head, but the coils of its body threshed the water and lashed at him with poisonous tentacles. Not until he had cut it into a hundred pieces was he sure that it was dead. Then he took Andromeda in his arms and flew with her to the shore. Cepheus and Cassiopeia embraced their daughter and gladly agreed that Perseus should marry her. There was feasting and rejoicing at the the wedding of the princess to the monster-slayer.

Before long Perseus's thoughts returned to Polydectes and the gift he bore him in the leather bag. Cepheus gave him a ship and a fine crew to carry him back to Seriphos with Andromeda. There they found preparations for another wedding. Polydectes had forced Danae to agree to marry him. Perseus found the king feasting with his cronies. They were sprawled around the table, shouting and calling for drink. The king was astounded to see Perseus in the doorway but he laughed.

'Here's the Gorgon-hunter back. Didn't you find her or didn't you look for her?'

'I found her' said Perseus, holding out the leather bag.

'Show me' bellowed Polydectes, not believing him.

'Show us,' roared the others, 'Show us the Gorgon's head!'

Perseus grasped the still-writhing serpents, drew the head from the bag and held it up. The jeers ceased. In stony silence Polydectes and his men sat at their banquet for ever.

Then Perseus and Andromeda ruled wisely in Seriphos and took care of Danae. However, not all the gods' intentions had been fulfilled. Perseus loved all kinds of sport. When a great competition was proclaimed in Thessaly he joined the men of many cities who took part. A great gathering formed to watch him throw the discus. Yet his throw, always so sure, this time veered from its course and struck an old man seated in the crowd. A cry arose from those around him. 'The king is dead! Acrisius is killed!' Thus the wicked old king was slain by the grandson he had never known and had believed long dead.

KING MIDAS AND THE GOLDEN TOUCH

Midas, king of Phrygia, was a most unhappy man. He had a prosperous kingdom and was rich, and yet he felt he should have been far richer. When he was a baby his nurse had seen a line of ants running across his cot; each insect had placed a grain of golden wheat in the little prince's mouth. The court soothsayers knew at once the meaning of this strange event – the golden grains were riches; one day Midas would be the richest king in the world.

When he grew up this promise of fantastic wealth obsessed the king. He wanted chests overflowing with gold and vast palaces filled with treasures from the corners of the earth. He wanted a mighty army to force neighbouring kings to bow to him; he wanted an empire. . . He wanted all these things – when would he get them? Time was running out. He began to think the gods would give him riches on the day he died.

One morning Midas was walking in his rose garden, imagining silver fountains and avenues of gold statues, when he saw a pair of hairy goat's feet sticking out from underneath a bush. They belonged to a satyr – one of those rascally creatures half man, half goat, who serve the wine god Dionysus. This satyr had been celebrating too well and had blundered into the royal garden to pass the night. He was flat on his back, fast asleep, with a garland of roses askew on his horns. Midas knew this uninvited visitor, though smelling rather goatish, must be treated with respect. He recognized him. It was old Silenus, who had been tutor to Dionysus when the wine god was a boy. Dionysus and Silenus still spent riotous days together. It would never do to offend Dionysus, so Midas told his gardeners to lift the satyr gently, put him in a wheelbarrow, and take him to the palace. 'Put him in the best guest-chamber and let him sleep it off.'

Silenus was never long the worse for wine. In a few hours he was

himself again. Midas ceremoniously invited him to share his midday meal. Lunching with Midas was usually a dreary affair – being so wrapped up in thoughts of gold, he found conversation difficult. With Silenus that was no problem. He did the talking. He had a fund of stories to make the gloomiest person grin. Midas was hugely entertained. 'Stay to supper,' he said.

Silenus had supper and enjoyed the fine wine. His bed was comfortable and the food was good. He was still there a week later when Dionysus came looking for him. The god had grown anxious about his old tutor. He was relieved to discover him very happy in a palace. Dionysus thanked Midas warmly. 'In return for your kindness to my servant, I will make you a gift. Name anything you wish.'

Anything he wished! Midas knew exactly what he wanted and unhesitatingly replied 'I wish everything I touch to turn to gold.'

Dionysus looked astonished. 'Is that really what you want' he asked. Midas assured him that nothing would make him happier. 'So be it then.' Dionysus said. He put an arm around Silenus and off they went.

Midas was left bewildered and excited. He could hardly believe his good luck. Untold wealth at last! His fingers itched to touch something yet he scarcely dared, for fear of disappointment. He broke a twig off an oak tree that grew beside the palace gate; instantly it became a twig of gold. He touched the gates. They turned to gold. Midas rushed back to the palace and touched the doors,

walls, the furniture. He had a palace all of gold! It was worth a fortune, and it was just a beginning. He would pave the streets of his capital with gold and ride in a golden chariot. No other king had wealth like this.

He commanded a celebration. 'Bring food and wine, and call the treasurer!' The treasurer blinked in amazement to see the room entirely changed to gold. 'I did it!' cried Midas. 'Look, I have the golden touch!' He put a finger on a pitcher of wine and the pitcher turned to gold. 'A toast to my kingdom's riches' he exclaimed, pouring wine into a cup that became gold as he handed it to the treasurer. The treasurer gulped the toast. Midas raised his own cup, but as the wine touched his lips it turned to liquid gold. He looked at it, appalled. A horrible suspicion struck him. He took bread from a dish and tried to break it; the loaf was solid gold. He bit a peach; it became gold. Every morsel of food and every drop of drink turned to gold on his lips. 'I shall starve to death,' he thought. 'No, no, I shall die of thirst long before that. How horrible!'

He fled to his bedchamber. Hungry, thirsty and very frightened, he put his head on his pillow and wept. But what a hard pillow - a rock of gold! During the night he dreamed that Dionysus came to him. 'Still unhappy, Midas?' he asked 'Haven't you enough gold?' 'Help me, lord Dionysus' Midas begged. 'Forgive my greed. Let me be like my poorest subject, but take this curse away.'

'Midas, you must learn to be reasonable in your wishes,' sighed the god. 'Poverty would not suit you, but tomorrow if you bathe in the spring where the River Pactolus rises from the ground, its waters will wash the golden touch away.'

The next day Midas stumbled along the river bank in his robes of woven gold. The climb was long and steep and the turf was hard and golden. Midas feared he was at his last gasp. He tore off his stiff, heavy clothes and went on naked. The spring formed a deep pool. Midas plunged in, let the waters close over him, and pulled himself out by an overhanging branch. Then he shouted for joy. The branch was green! The golden touch was gone. The turf was green again, he was himself again, a king like any other. But the sands of the River Pactolus are bright to this day with flecks of gold.

THESEUS AND THE MINOTAUR

King Minos ruled the island of Crete in the midst of the blue Mediterranean Sea. It was a happy land; its people were successful traders; its countryside produced good wine and fat sheep and goats; its king was powerful and feared by other nations. And yet King Minos seemed anything but happy. Day by day his expression grew more grim. Rumours began to spread about the court that Minos had some terrible secret.

One day King Minos summoned his wisest advisers. 'I wish to build a new palace,' he said. 'Not an ordinary palace. I want a palace of an unimaginable kind. Who is the architect I need?'

'Without doubt you need Daedalus of Athens,' said the advisers. 'He is the most cunning of craftsmen, and an inventor of wonders. He makes machines that walk and statues that can speak.'

So Daedalus was summoned to Crete and built the king a palace of such a kind that no one had seen its like. It had no outside windows. The rooms within were a mystery, for Daedalus had been sworn to secrecy.

When it was finished Minos looked at it with grim approval.

'Now, build a wall around it. Not one wall. I want many walls. Crooked walls with many turnings.'

Daedalus was astonished but he did as he was ordered, surrounding the building with row upon row of high walls. The dark passages between them made a gigantic maze.

Now what was the reason for this maze? The king and his wife Pasiphae had been unwise enough to make an enemy of the great sea god Poseidon. They had broken a solemn promise to honour him with the sacrifice of a magical bull sent to them from the sea. Instead they had kept the animal for themselves. Poseidon was enraged and caused poor Pasiphae to give birth to a hideous beast, the Minotaur, half man, half bull. Minos, though obliged to accept the monster as his son, was determined to keep it hidden from sight. He had devised this prison for it, a palace from which it could never escape and into which no prying person could find the way.

But the secret of the Minotaur could not be kept for long. As it grew up the beast proved terrifyingly savage. It soon began demanding human flesh to eat. Minos declared that all the conquered cities that paid him tax should in future send healthy young people to feed the Minotaur. From Athens he demanded seven youths and seven maidens, to be paid every ninth year.

Aegeus, the king of Athens, was a weak man who only bewailed the calamity. Twice the terrible payment was made, accompanied by hopeless weeping as the young people sailed for Crete in a boat carrying a black sail. In the year that the third payment fell due a stranger arrived at the Athenian court - a young man, Aegeus's unknown son Theseus. When he heard the story of the seven youths and maidens he bravely demanded to go as one of them, to kill the Minotaur. His father was dismayed at the thought of losing his new-found son, but he yielded at last. Aegeus asked his son to promise one thing.

'If you return victorious,' he said, 'order the black sail to be lowered and raise a white one. Then I shall know at once that you are safe.' And Theseus promised that he would.

Watching the horizon, the young Athenians saw the island of Crete appear, and looked at it with dread. But they had a shred of hope, for no one who saw Theseus could doubt that he was a favourite of the gods, both for his courage and his beauty. Minos's daughter Ariadne thought so, when she saw him leading the young Athenians to the king. Even Minos was unwilling to fling such a noble prince to the monster. He urged him to think again and go home. Theseus laughed at this suggestion.

'Then you must be my guest for a fortnight and I will sacrifice you last' said Minos. But Theseus insisted that he should be the first to meet the monster.

Minos grew irritated. 'If that's your wish,' he said, 'tomorrow you can get to know him well.' That night the princess Ariadne tiptoed to the room where Theseus lay and whispered, 'I want to save you. But if I help you, you must swear to take me to Athens with you as your wife, for my father will kill me when he learns what I have done.'

Theseus readily agreed. Ariadne gave him a sword which she had obtained from Daedalus, and told him what the cunning Athenian had advised. 'This sword is the only weapon that can harm the monster. Take it, and take this ball of thread to guide you through the maze.' Then in the dark she led him to the entrance to the maze, tied the end of the thread to the huge ring in the centre of the door and told him to always keep the ball in his hand.

Theseus felt his way cautiously in the dark. He would have wandered aimlessly if the thread had not shown him the ways he had already taken. He had unrolled the last of the thread when he heard ahead of him a steady pounding. The Minotaur was pacing round and

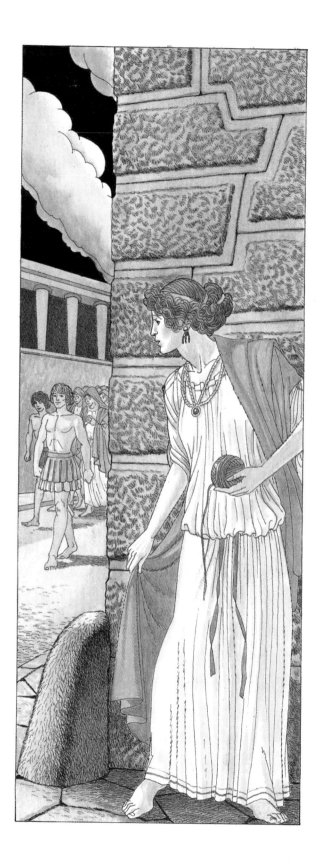

round in some open space, quite close to him. The moment had come. Theseus stepped into the dim light of a courtyard. The Minotaur saw him and charged. Theseus darted aside and swung the sword with all his force into the creature's belly. With a bellow of rage the monster fell to the ground, grasping Theseus so that he fell upon it. He felt the soft skin underneath its throat and drove the sword in deep. The monster groaned and died.

Shaken but triumphant, Theseus followed the thread back to Ariadne who was waiting at the gate. She flung her arms around him, then through the sleeping city she guided the Athenians to the harbour. They stole aboard their ship and sailed for Athens. During the voyage they sheltered for the night upon the island of Naxos. Next day, when Ariadne awoke, she found herself alone. The ship had sailed without her. Some say that Theseus had never loved her and had left her on the island. But others tell how the wine god Dionysus had come to him that night in a dream and commanded him to go. This surely is the truth, for while Ariadne wept, Dionysus, with his band of laughing satyrs, came tumbling from the sky and carried her off to be his wife.

Theseus sailed on, and sorrow for Ariadne made him forget to put up the white sail as ·he had promised. Aegeus, who had gone every day to the cliff top to watch for his son's boat, saw the black sail returning and cast himself into the sea for grief. So Theseus came home to mourning and became king of Athens, which he ruled long and well.

DAEDALUS AND ICARUS

Great was the wrath of King Minos when he learned that the Minotaur lay dead and the Athenians had fled with his daughter. The Minotaur had been a torment to him, but to find him killed was dishonouring to the king and to the people of Crete. Whom could he blame? His suspicions immediately fell on Daedalus.

Daedalus was dragged before the throne. The king eyed him grimly.

'You have served me even in your treachery, by building your own prison,' he said. So Daedalus was locked in the Minotaur's desolate palace together with his son Icarus, a boy of ten, for the king had sworn to have no more Athenians living on the island of Crete.

Daedalus blamed himself bitterly for the dismal life his son led without friends or any smiling faces to see. He tried to make up for this by telling the boy stories and making him mechanical toys, but Daedalus's sad face belied his cheerful words. Icarus would find his father gazing from the palace's high tower, far out over the sea. 'Athens lies that way, Icarus,' he would say and point, and Icarus would feel grieved for his father.

Whenever his father's sadness made him silent, Icarus climbed to the top of the tower and called to the sea birds circling overhead. He was trying to train them to take bread from his hands. If he stood still long enough they would perch on his arm or his head, but as soon as he tried to catch one it spread its wings and was off. 'Why does it do that?' he complained to his father. 'Why do they always fly away?'

'Who would not fly from here if they had wings? said his father bitterly. Then, 'Wings!' he repeated in quite a different tone. 'Why not? It must be possible. It would be the most stupendous of all my inventions.'

From then on Daedalus set Icarus to search every day for feathers dropped by the birds - strong tail feathers and soft, curly down from the breast – and made him sort them into types and sizes. It took a year to get enough for Daedalus's invention to start taking shape. He made a wooden framework and mounted the feathers on it, row on row, placing each feather in melted wax which set and held it firm. He shaped the rows in curves to form a wing. Icarus watched him, hard at work, with some dismay. He did not want to hurt his father's feelings but felt himself too grown up for dressing up in feathers like a bird. But when the wings were finished they were broad and long like an eagle's – two pairs of them – and their span was wider by far than Icarus's outstretched arms. Daedalus showed

his son how to thread his arms through the straps beneath the wings, and bound the leather harness round his chest. Then he did the same for himself. 'Raise your arms like this,' he told Icarus, 'and again, like this.'

Already Icarus could feel the air lifting him a little from the ground. He glided across the roof and might have stepped beyond if his father had not caught him by the heels and dragged him back.

'We are going on a journey, Icarus' Daedalus said with a stern face. 'Listen carefully. When I open my wings, open your own and follow me. The air will carry us, never fear. But at all times you must keep close beside me. We must not fly too low or the sea mists will clog our feathers, nor too high or the sun will melt the wax that holds them. Now, if you are ready, we shall say farewell to Minos and this hateful tower for ever'

Icarus promised faithfully to stay near his father. Daedalus, with tears in his eyes, kissed his son and hugged him, and said 'Now – jump, after me!'

Icarus, never for a moment doubting his father, stepped out into the air. Not raising his arms quite soon enough, he saw for one horrible second the walls of the maze apparently rushing towards his feet. Then as his wings beat the air he rose again, up and out, far above the imprisoning walls of the palace and over the countryside. Ploughmen in the fields looked up and thought they saw two huge birds overhead. Grape pickers dropped their baskets and shaded their eyes – for surely those were men with wings?

Villagers called to their chldren to come and see the gods in flight.

Daedalus showed Icarus how to tack and veer to keep a course north-west towards Greece. They passed the shoreline, where Minos's beached warships looked like toys left on the sand. Now they were out over the open sea. Icarus saw the sea birds far below him. 'I am up with the eagles,' he thought, 'not down there with the gulls.' With a few strokes of his wings he soared even higher, quite forgetting his father's warning. What space there was around him! The sea was a dim haze far below and the sun felt warm on his back. 'Look at *me*!' he called to the empty air. He swooped and soared, higher and still higher. 'I could reach the stars and not be tired. No bird has ever been as high as this.' And yet he noticed there were feathers in the air. More were fluttering from him as he flew. The sun was melting the wax and his feathers were slipping from their wooden frame. Frantically he beat his arms up and down in the air. It was no longer a cushion bearing him along, but a vast hollow through which he dropped like a stone into the sea. In vain he called for his father to save him. The waves closed over him and he was drowned.

Daedalus, searching desperately for his son, found only feathers floating on the ocean. He wept bitter tears and cursed his own cleverness for causing his son's death. Then he spread his wings and flew towards his homeland, to pass his days in grief.

THE TWELVE LABOURS OF HERACLES

Perseus founded a great family known as the Perseids, who were princes of Argos. His favourite grandchild was Alcmene, whom Zeus loved. Zeus' queen, Hera, grew frantically jealous when she learned that Alcmene was expecting a child.

Zeus, highly delighted, declared before all the gods that the very next child to be born to the Perseids was destined to be king of Argos. But Hera bribed the goddess of childbirth to delay the birth of Alcmene's child and bring forward that of a baby cousin. So this cousin, named Eurystheus, grew up to be king of Argos, though he was a feeble, chicken-hearted creature. Alcmene's son became the most famous of the heroes – the tallest, strongest, and boldest. His name was Heracles, though he is better known by the name the Romans gave him – Hercules.

Hera sent two poisonous serpents by night to baby Heracles to destroy him. The sturdy infant sat up in his cradle, seized a serpent in each fist and strangled it. His crows of glee awoke his mother. Such unheard-of strength and daring in a child proved beyond doubt his father was a god. Hera's anger was more bitter than before.

Revenge is a dish that can be eaten cold. Hera was prepared to wait, for the greater Heracles' reputation grew the more she would relish destroying it. As a boy he outstripped all others in strength and courage. The fire in his eyes was god-like, and his temper was god-like too. Yet everything Heracles did he did well. His bow and spear never missed their mark; he was skilled in music, astronomy and philosophy. He rid Argos of many troublesome creatures – bears, wolves, fiery serpents – that plagued it. In gratitude for this help the king of Thebes gave Heracles his daughter Megara as a bride, and six sons were born to them. Then Hera sent a fit of madness to Heracles, and mistaking his young sons for enemies, he killed them all.

When he regained his sanity Heracles shut himself alone in a dark room for days. Finally he visited Apollo's oracle at Delphi and asked what he must do to be forgiven. The oracle ordered him to become Eurystheus's servant and do whatever tasks his cousin set.

Heracles loathed the thought of serving a man he despised. Yet the gods must be obeyed, so he presented himself at Mycenae, the stronghold of the kings of Argos. King Eurystheus gloated at the thought of controlling his great cousin. 'You must perform ten labours for me,' he declared, 'First bring me the body of the Nemean lion.'

This lion, an enormous beast with a hide that neither iron nor bronze nor stone could pierce, was devouring the people of Nemea. Heracles seized it by the throat and choked it to death. He skinned it by using its own claws to cut its hide, and ever after wore the hide as armour, with its gaping jaws as a helmet. Dressed like this he re-entered Mycenae. Eurystheus was terrified. 'Next time stay outside the gates' he said. 'For your next labour you must kill the hydra of Lerna – but you can leave its body behind – I don't want to see it here.'

The hydra was a many-headed water snake that lurked in the swamp of Lerna. It had possessed nine heads, but when one was cut off two immediately grew in its place. Heracles' sword only multiplied the heads, so he shouted to his chariot driver, Iolaus, for help. Iolaus set fire to a forest and seared the Hydra's wounds with burning wood, so that the blood dried and no new heads could grow.

'I shall not count that labour' declared Eurystheus. 'Iolaus helped. Now bring me back the Erymanthian boar.'

This was a monstrous animal that lived on Mount Erymanthus. Heracles drove it into a snow-drift, leapt on its back and overpowered it. Eurystheus was so frightened at its appearance that he hid in a big bronze jar sunk in the ground. 'Now,' he said from the bottom of the jar, 'you must catch the golden-antlered Ceryneian hind.'

The hind was a magical beast sacred to Artemis. It was astonishingly swift, even for a deer, hiding in the thickets of rocky Mount Ceryneia. Heracles pursued it for a year without catching it, but finally it fell exhausted. He clasped its slender legs together and carried it to Mycenae. But Eurystheus could not keep it. Directly its feet touched the ground it was off again, never to be recaught.

'Now clean out the stables of King Augeias,' said Eurystheus. 'In one day.'

Augeias, king of Elis, had such vast herds of cattle that their dung filled their stables and overflowed into the countryside. The fields were so deep in dung the cattle could not feed. Heracles made a bargain with Augeias. He would clear the dung for a tenth of the cattle. He broke down the wall of the yard in two places and diverted two rivers so that they swept through the stables and went on to wash the pastures clean. But Augeias refused to pay him the cattle. He said the river gods had done the work.

'I'm not counting that as a labour' said Eurystheus, when Heracles got back. 'You were hired by Augeias so you weren't working for me.' So Heracles got the worst of both worlds.

For the next five labours Hercules got rid of a flock of brass-feathered man-eating birds which were breeding in the Stymphalian Marsh, captured a fire-breathing bull that was ravaging Crete, fetched the golden girdle of Queen Hippolyta of the Amazons, and brought back the cattle of Geryon the triple-bodied from the island of Erythia. He then tamed the four savage mares of King Diomedes, which were kept tethered by iron chains to bronze mangers and were fed on the flesh of unsuspecting visitors. Heracles fed the king to his own horses, and when they were no longer hungry he managed them with ease. He then said he had done ten labours and demanded his release.

Eurystheus was by now so terrified of Heracles and his booty that he stayed in his jar and communicated with Heracles through a herald. Though the king was a coward he knew he had Hera on his side. 'I make it eight labours' he said. 'Go and fetch Cerberus

from the underworld.'

Eurystheus never dreamt that Heracles would do this, but down he went fearlessly to the underworld and asked Hades to loan him Cerberus, the three-headed dog that guarded his gates. Hades said Heracles could have him if he could catch him without using a weapon. Heracles gripped the dog by his single throat. His serpent tail flew up to strike but could not pierce Heracles' lion-skin armour. Heracles slipped a chain round his neck and dragged him up to the light. Eurystheus was scared to look at him. 'Bring me some golden apples from the Garden of the Hesperides,' he said.

These apples had been a wedding gift to Hera from Gaia, Mother Earth. Hera had planted them in her Garden of the West, where they grew on a tree guarded by a dragon and tended by the three Hesperides, daughters of the Evening Star. Heracles had to discover how to get there. He went to consult Nereus, the Old Man of the Sea, who

could take whatever shape he wished. He found the old sea-god asleep in a cave, grabbed him by the beard and held on tight. Nereus turned into a serpent, then into fire, then water, but Heracles clung on and forced him to reveal the way to the garden. 'Do not go in,' warned Nereus. 'You must ask someone else to pick the apples.'

Heracles came to the garden where the Hesperides danced before the apple tree but did not take a step inside. He went instead to Atlas, the Titan who stood by the entrance bearing the whole weight of the sky on his head, and offered to carry it for a moment if Atlas would get the apples for him. Atlas agreed gladly and came back with an armful of apples. Shedding his burden had been such joy that he volunteered to take the apples to Eurystheus himself if Heracles would hold the sky a while longer. Heracles saw where that would lead. He pretended to agree, asking Atlas to take the weight for a second while he put a cushion on his head. Simple-minded Atlas took the sky again and Heracles thanked him and was off.

Eurystheus could not deny that the labours were now complete. The gods, watching from Olympus, tried to persuade Hera to relent. 'Had it not been for you, none of these great deeds would have come about, so Heracles has glorified your name.' And in time she forgave him.

This is not even a tenth of the many tales of Heracles, whom Zeus finally created a god. All the Olympians welcomed him and Hera adopted him as her son.

THE STORY OF PHAETON

Phaeton was a boy with a mop of hair like a sunburst and an eager shining face. When he was six or seven years old, and school friends asked each other, 'What does your father do?' Phaeton would answer, 'My father is Helios the sun god,' and it seemed a reasonable answer at the time.

But as they grew older his friends began asking questions.

'What does your father look like?' and 'When does he visit you?'

Phaeton had to confess that he had never seen his father. 'He is too busy driving the sun's chariot,' he said.

'He doesn't drive all night. You're only boasting. Your father's really some worn-out sailor, stranded at Assus with no boat to bring him back.'

'The sun god is my father. He is, he is, he is!' cried Phaeton.

'How do you know?

'My mother told me so.'

At this they burst out laughing and made fun of him. Phaeton was furious. He stalked away and went to find his mother.

'Why do we never see my father here?' he asked her.

His mother, a sad-eyed woman called Clymene, looked surprised.

'How could your father come to us? she asked. 'Helios is a great god, with many tasks to do. He cannot trouble himself with our concerns.'

'But I must have some proof he is my father. You say he is, but that's no good at all.'

Clymene's face grew sadder. 'Isn't my word enough for you?' she asked.

Phaeton hung his golden head and looked ashamed and sulky. He did not answer yes.

'Go to the sun god, then,' said Clymene. 'Ask him yourself whether he is your father. Beyond the eastern mountains you will find the palace of the sun. Go there and see how he will answer you.'

Phaeton was delighted to be sent on such a journey. 'That will give the others something to think about,' he thought, 'when they learn where I've gone.' He journeyed eastwards over the mountains, towards the sunrise, until he reached the golden palace of the sun. It sat aloft among the clouds on glittering golden columns, with a roof of ivory and silver doors. Phaeton feared he could never reach it, but unseen hands raised him up so that he stood before the palace gates. He passed boldly through the lofty entrance into the hall of the sun god.

Helios, in a purple robe, sat on a throne bright with shining emeralds. Beside him stood the Days, some smiling, some with cloudy faces, some in tears. In front of them the Hours danced round and round in a circle, never stopping. The Years and their Seasons were in attendance too, Summer's face blazed and Winter's hair sparkled with silver frost. The scene was almost too dazzling for Phaeton's eyes to bear, but he remembered that he was claiming kinship with the gods and forced himself to look at Helios and kneel before his throne.

The sun god, whose eye sees everything, had seen the boy upon his journey and was expecting him. 'Never doubt, Phaeton, that you are my son,' he said with a smile of welcome. 'You needed courage to come here. I am proud of you.' Then Helios laid aside the rays that gleamed around his head and embraced his son. 'You have come far to see me and I would like to give you something in return,' he said. 'Name what

you wish and you shall have it.'

Phaeton's heart swelled with happiness. He felt like a prince. He replied eagerly 'Let me drive your chariot across the sky, father.'

Helios shook his head, 'Anything but that,' he said. 'Such a task is far beyond your strength. Not even the gods, not Zeus himself can drive the sun's chariot. No one but I can manage its fiery horses and hold them to their course. Choose something else, my son.'

'But father, you promised.'

Phaeton would not let slip this wonderful chance. Nothing that Helios could say would make him change his mind. A promise was a promise, so with the greatest reluctance Helios helped his son to mount the golden chariot and placed the sun's rays on his head. Dawn flung open the gates of the new day and Phaeton grasped the reins tightly and was off.

The sun's fire-breathing horses hurled themselves upwards along the arched pathway of the sky. At once they missed the firm hand of the sun god on the reins. They scented freedom and galloped where they wished, churning the clouds up with their hooves. Phaeton was panic-stricken. He did not know the way; he did not even know the horses' names. The chariot plunged and swayed as if it were empty, at one moment near the earth, the next far from it. The arctic regions of the world grew hot; the tropics shuddered under icy winds and snow.

Then Phaeton saw the terrible inhabitants of the sky looming about him, the scorpion with its great claws and poisonous sting and other creatures of the zodiac. Horrified, he shut his eyes and dropped the reins. The horses then grew frantic. With nothing to restrain them they dashed themselves against the stars, dried up the clouds and dragged the chariot down until it almost grazed the mountains. Green lands were turned to desert and the rivers boiled. The earth caught fire, cities were burned and entire nations perished.

Zeus saw with horror that the world was burning. To save mankind he hurled a thunderbolt at Phaeton, whose flaming body fell like a star into the river Eridanus, and was cool at last. Helios was grief-stricken and hid himself, so that for a whole day the world was dark. Clymene, wandering the earth to find her son's body, discovered it at last beside the river, buried by the nymphs.

THE WOODEN HORSE

This is the tale of how Greeks and Trojans became deadly enemies and battled for ten long years, and how victory was finally won through a trick. The gods took sides, many men died and a great city was burned - all for the sake of a woman, the most beautiful the world has ever seen.

It began with a wedding. The sea nymph Thetis was to marry a mortal, Peleus, a prince of Thessaly. Zeus had arranged the marriage himself and invited all the gods to the feast - all except Eris, the goddess of discord, whose presence was not wanted. However, she came unasked, and without saying anything tossed a golden apple into the midst of the guests and disappeared. The apple bore the words, "For the fairest". At once the three most beautiful goddesses, Hera, Athene and Aphrodite, tried to seize it, each claiming it was meant for her. A bitter quarrel broke out. Zeus declared that he would appoint an umpire who knew nothing of the quarrel. He chose a handsome shepherd boy named Paris who tended his flocks far away across the sea, on the slopes of Mount Ida in Phrygia - not far from the great city of Troy.

Hermes, carrying the apple, accompanied the goddesses to Paris and told him to give the apple to the most beautiful. Before the astonished young man had time to decide, the goddesses began to offer bribes. Hera offered him power; if he chose her he would rule over vast kingdoms. Athene offered wisdom and victory; he would never be defeated in battle. Aphrodite promised love; she would give him the most beautiful woman in the world - Helen, wife of King Menelaus of Sparta. Without hesitation, Paris gave Aphrodite the golden apple. The whole world knew of Helen's wondrous beauty; all the princes of Greece had been her suitors, ready to kill each other out of jealousy. To prevent bloodshed her guardian had extorted a promise that, if Helen freely chose one of them,

the others would support him against anyone who challenged his right to be her husband. Helen had chosen Menelaus.

The rage of Hera and Athene at being rejected knew no bounds. They became deadly enemies of Paris, while Aphrodite did her utmost to protect him. Paris was the son of Priam, king of Troy, who was now an old man with many sons and daugters. When Paris was born it had been foretold that he would cause the ruin of his father's kingdom. To prevent this calamity, Priam had given orders that the baby should be left upon a hillside to die. But the infant Paris was found by a shepherd who rescued him and brought him up. Aphrodite now restored him to his family and Priam, who had long repented his action, received his son with joy. On the sea shore outside the walls of Troy Paris built a fine ship, and under Aphrodite's protection set sail to find the reward she had promised him.

Menelaus, quite unsuspecting, made Paris welcome as an honoured guest. After a few days the king had to make a journey, and left his wife to entertain the Trojan traveller. Then Paris easily persuaded Helen, who was under the spell of Aphrodite, to run away with him. They fled to his ship and a favourable wind blew them swiftly across the sea to Troy.

When it was known that a Trojan had seized and carried off the wife of King Menelaus the Greeks were furiously angry and swore that she must be brought back. This was no easy matter, for the Trojans would not let her go, and they were secure within the strong walls of Troy. The anger of the Greeks might have cooled had it not been for their greatest warrior - King Agamemnon of Mycenae, brother of Menelaus. He reminded the Greek leaders of the vow they had made to support Helen's husband. 'Now is the time,' he urged, 'to honour that vow.' The mightiest Greek kings and warriors, with all the armed followers they could raise, sailed in a huge fleet to attack Troy.

Troy stood in a wide plain beside the sea. Priam had entrusted its defence to his eldest son Hector, a brave and honourable prince. Hector led the Trojans to the shore to prevent the Greeks landing, but so many men poured from the boats that the Trojans were forced, with heavy fighting, to retreat within the walls of Troy. They barred its massive gate. The triumphant Greeks encamped along the shore, but hopes of an easy victory proved false. For nine long years they besieged the city, for nine years the Trojans kept them

out. Many bloody battles were fought on the Trojan plain. In the tenth year the Greek leaders began to quarrel, and men talked openly of going home. At a council of war the cunning Odysseus, king of Ithaca, suggested a plan. 'We break our swords in vain against Troy's walls' he said. 'Be guided by me and I will show you how the city may be taken.'

When the Trojan watchmen looked out from the city walls at dawn next day the Greek tents had vanished from the plain; no ships lay along the shore. The unbelievable had happened; the Greeks had given up and sailed for home. The news spread throughout the city and men, women and children streamed out of the gates rejoicing. On the shore where the Greeks had camped they found the strangest object - an enormous wooden horse. Its legs were like trees; its huge head was beyond the reach of the tallest man. At once the crowd began to argue over what this terrible object meant. 'It is an offering to the gods,' said some. 'The Greeks have left it for Athene who favours them.' 'Then let us take it into the city,' cried others, 'and honour Athene with offerings to the horse, and turn the Greeks' own gift against them.' But Laocoon, a priest of Poseidon, who had come with his two sons to beg the sea god to raise a storm and drown the Greek fleet, denounced the idea. 'Fools!' said Laocoon. 'Do you not know Greek cunning? I fear them even when they leave us gifts. We must destroy the horse.' And he hurled his spear at its wooden flank which

reverberated with a hollow sound.

At that moment a Greek was discovered amongst the rocks, his hands bound behind him. To the Trojans' questions he replied that the Greeks had indeed abandoned the siege and left; the horse was an offering to Athene to ensure a safe journey home. He, a condemned man, had been intended as a sacrifice, but he had escaped and hidden in the rocks.

'But why did the Greeks build so huge a horse?' he was asked.

'To stop it entering Troy's gate' the captive replied. 'Our soothsayer warned that if the horse were brought into the city, Troy would enjoy the protection of the gods for ever.'

While the people hesitated, a strange noise came from the sea, a sound like the boiling of the ocean, and two huge serpents emerged from the waves. The heavy coils of their bodies snaked across the shore to wrap themselves around Laocoon's sons. The horrified father went to their rescue, but was at once entrapped. All three were squeezed

to death. The Trojans saw at once that some mighty god resented Laocoon's treatment of the horse. Their minds made up, they took down the stone lintel of the great gate to allow the horse to be hauled in. A great procession escorted the horse to the heart of the city, where the people garlanded it with flowers, and danced, and feasted and drank wine in its honour.

When the happy Trojans finally slept, a trapdoor in the belly of the horse swung open and fifty armed Greeks dropped to the ground. Some raced to the gate, overcame the guards and let in the Greek army, which under cover of darkness had sailed back from the headland where it had hidden. Others fired the town, which blazed all night. The unarmed Trojans were slaughtered and their women taken as slaves. Thus by a trick the long war ended in one night. Old Priam was killed and Troy was utterly destroyed. Paris was dead and Helen, for whose sake all this was done, shed not a single tear. She returned to Menelaus and sailed with him for Greece.

THE WANDERINGS OF ODYSSEUS

Troy was burnt and the war was over. After ten years the Greeks longed for home. Odysseus commanded his men to stock their boats with all the food and wine and treasure from Troy that they could cram in. Then they set out to sea for Ithaca. Almost at once a fierce gale drove them into unknown seas. After nine hard days they put into an island for water. Odysseus and twelve companions went ashore to explore, taking wine with them as a friendly offering to the unknown people of the land.

This island was home to the Cyclops, slow-witted, lumbering giants of tremendous strength; they had only one eye, set in their foreheads. Odysseus and his men came to a deep cave full of barrels of milk and huge cheeses. They were about to make off with as much as they could carry when they heard a heavy tread which made the rocks around them shake. The owner of the cave was returning, a Cyclops called Polyphemus, the most savage of them all. Poseidon was Polyphemus's father and even he could not control him.

Odysseus and his men ran behind the barrels as the giant entered the cave. He was driving a flock of sheep before him, to shelter for the night. Under his arm he had a bundle of tree trunks. He flung a couple of these on the embers of a fire, blew on it to make a blaze, and rolled a gigantic slab of rock across the mouth of the cave to close it. Then he squatted down to milk his sheep. He filled a huge pail with milk and drank it at a gulp, then another and another. Then he saw Odysseus and his men hiding in the shadows. With a great roar he demanded to know what they were doing there.

Odysseus stepped forward. 'We are poor sailors cast up on your island. We seek only a little food and shelter which we trust you will allow us in the name of hospitality, as is pleasing to the gods.'

Polyphemus replied by seizing two of Odysseus's men by the heels with one hand, smashing their heads against the wall of the cave and eating them, bones and all.

The Greeks dared not move or speak, each expecting to be the next mouthful. But Polyphemus was full now and sleepy. He brushed some sheep aside with back of his hand to clear a space, stretched himself out on the floor and was soon snoring loudly.

'Let's run him through with our swords while he sleeps,' whispered one of the men.

'What help would that be?' said Odysseus. 'We can't shift that stone from the entrance. We would be trapped.' Their plight seemed hopeless. They could do nothing.

The next morning two more unfortunate Greeks were eaten for Polyphemus's breakfast. Then he took his sheep out to graze, rolling the rock back after him to shut the Greeks inside. Cunning Odysseus and his men dragged a tree trunk out of the giant's woodpile and shaved one end to a sharp point with their swords. Then they hid the pointed stake at the back of the cave.

The giant came back at night and milked his flock and crunched two men for his supper as before. Then Odysseus stepped forward with a cup of the wine brought from the ship.

'Drink this, great Cyclops,' he said. 'You may like it better than milk.'

Polyphemus emptied the bowl in one gulp. 'More!' he said. Odysseus refilled the cup. The Cyclops was unused to wine. Instead of feeling furious, he felt that life was good. 'I like you

a lot,' he told Odysseus. 'It's a pity to eat you. I'll save you to the last. What is your name?'

'My name is Nobody,' replied Odysseus.

'Funny name!' said the giant, blinking stupidly and swaying. He got to his feet uncertainly, kicked the rock across the entrance, fell flat on his back in front of it and immediately started to snore.

Odysseus and his men got the stake and heated its point red-hot in the fire. Then they drove the burning point into the Cyclops's eye and twisted it about. Polyphemus gave a horrible yell which brought the other Cyclopes running. 'Is someone in there with you? Who is it?' they shouted.

'Nobody's in here! Nobody's to blame!' bellowed Polyphemus from inside the cave.

'Well if it's nobody's fault we can't do much' said the others, and went off again.

In the morning blind Polyphemus rolled back the rock to let his sheep out, but he felt each one to make sure that it was a sheep and not a man. Odysseus told his men to grab the wool of a sheep's belly and hang

on underneath. Polyphemus ran his hands over the back of each sheep but never thought of feeling below, so Odysseus and his remaining men escaped. They ran to the ships, driving as many sheep as possible on board, and at once set sail.

Looking shoreward, Odysseus saw the sightless giant stumbling over the rocks and called: 'For your cruelty to strangers, the gods have punished you, and it is I, Odysseus of Ithaca, who have done it for them.'

Polyphemus tore a giant boulder out of the earth and hurled it at the taunting voice. It hit the water just behind the vessel, raising a wave that almost swamped the ship. Then Polyphemus prayed to Poseidon 'Grant, father, that my enemy Odysseus may never reach home, or if he must, let it be after years of woes and may he find nothing but trouble waiting for him.' Poseidon heard and promised vengeance.

A terrible storm immediately beset Odysseus's ship. It blew it to the island of Aeolus, Lord of the Winds. Aeolus listened to Odysseus's misfortunes and gave him a bulging leather bag, closed tight with a cord. 'This is the bag of all the winds,' Aeolus said. 'Let the west wind out of the bag and it will blow you home.' Odysseus thanked him warmly and set off again. Opening the bag a little way he let out enough wind to speed the ship towards Ithaca. He steered night and day, keeping the bag by his side and letting no one near it. The coast of Ithaca was just on the horizon when he fell asleep exhausted. His men, thinking the

bag held treasure which Odysseus did not mean to share, cut the cord while he slept. All the winds rushed out and roared homeward, driving the ship back to Aeolus.

Aeolus refused to help any more. 'Poseidon is against you and I dare not' he said. So the battered ship put to sea again. After many days the crew landed on a fair island. Odysseus sent men to discover who owned the place. In the midst of a wood they came to a palace before which lions and wolves were prowling, but instead of attacking, the beasts licked their hands and seemed to wish to tell them something. They were greeted by a beautiful woman who welcomed them and invited them to eat. No sooner had the famished sailors touched food than she struck them with her wand. They fell on all fours and became a herd of pigs, which she drove into stinking sties.

One man, too cautious to enter the palace, escaped to tell Odysseus, who seized his sword and rushed to save his men. On his

way he was met by a stranger who warned him to be less hasty, for they were in the power of Circe, a powerful enchantress. The stranger proved to be the god Hermes, who gave Odysseus a charm against Circe's magic, a little white flower that grew wild on the island. Odysseus put it in the drink that Circe offered him. Then he put his sword to her throat, threatening to kill her if she did not at once restore her victims to their proper shape. She was forced to undo her magic and turn lions, wolves and pigs to men again.

But all was not yet well. Circe had fallen in love with the bold and clever Odysseus, and her beauty was enough to persuade him, without any magic, to stay on the island. He spent a year in her pleasure palace, and might have stayed longer if his men had not begun to grumble mutinously.

Then Odysseus came to his senses and set sail once more. He had many many ordeals ahead of him - Poseidon saw to that. In the tenth year of his wanderings Odysseus was washed overboard and cast up on the shores of generous King Alcinous who dispatched a ship which brought Odysseus to Ithaca at last. The king's servants laid him, fast asleep, upon the beach and left him there.

THE HOMECOMING OF ODYSSEUS

Twenty years is a long time to be away from home. As the years passed most of Odysseus's people forgot him, or believed him dead. His son Telemachus had been a baby when he left and never knew him. Only his wife Penelope continually thought of him and did not give up hope that he was alive and would return.

As the years passed the nobles of Odysseus's realm began to cast greedy looks at the throne. Telemachus was still a boy, and Penelope had no one to protect her. Since Odysseus must be dead, whoever married Penelope would be king. Each of these ambitious men distrusted the others, and each came himself to the palace to woo Penelope. No fewer than a hundred and eight suitors turned up, and said they would stay until Penelope had chosen one of them as a husband. They were arrogant and boisterous, drinking Odysseus's wine and killing his herds for their feasts. This broke all rules of courtesy, for as suitors they should have brought splendid presents for Penelope and each put on a feast for all the others at their own expense. Penelope despised and feared these shameless spongers. Yet she could not make them leave.

To keep the suitors good humoured, she promised to choose a husband when she had finished weaving the cloth on her loom. Every day she worked at her loom, every night she secretly undid all that she had done during the day. For three years she kept the suitors waiting, until they grew suspicious and bribed a maid to follow her. Then her trick was discovered. 'Now choose a husband,' they said, 'and let there be a king in Ithaca.'

But Penelope would not choose. Then the suitors began to look evilly at Telemachus who would soon be old enough to throw them out. Hearing he had sailed in search of his father, they planned to waylay his ship and murder him as he returned.

And so it happened that while Odysseus slept upon the beach in Ithaca, his son was sailing home into an ambush. The goddess Athene saw it all and stepped in to sort matters out. Only respect for her uncle Poseidon had prevented her from spiriting Odysseus home long before. Now she awoke him as he lay on the shore, and warned him of the suitors and of Penelope's plight. She guided him to a swineherd's hut and united him there with Telemachus, whom she had warned to sail home by another route. Telemachus was overjoyed to be told this was his father home again. Advised by Athene, the two made plans. Athene transformed Odysseus into a withered and decrepit old beggar so that he could enter the palace unknown. He and Telemachus would wait to rid themselves of the suitors, knowing Athene would provide them with an opportunity to do so.

Not a single person at the palace recognized the old beggar. But there was one loving heart that could not be deceived. On the threshold lay Odysseus's old dog Argos, who had been a fine hunting dog when he went away. The old hound lifted its mangy head and wagged the raw stump of its tail. It knew its master was home once more. And so, contented at last, it died. Odysseus brushed away a tear at seeing it and entered the palace.

Telemachus, pretending not to know the beggar, offered him shelter, as it was right to do to all strangers. But the suitors were rude and scornful. Odysseus began to beg some food from each in turn, to learn what sort of men they were. They all proved mean and gave him little, and arrogant Antinous, the worst of them, threw a stool at him. Penelope was scandalized at this treatment of a stranger. She ordered her servants to care for him and provide him with a bed, and called her old maidservant, Eurycleia, to bathe his feet. Eurycleia had nursed Odysseus when he was a boy. Already the beggar reminded her of her lost master, but when she washed his legs and recognized a scar above his knee she knew this was Odysseus. She spilled the water, for her eyes were full of tears. Odysseus swore her to silence.

That night Penelope came to a decision. She had learned of the suitors' plot against Telemachus and knew that they would try again. To protect her son's life she resolved she would have to marry one of them. At dawn she rose and took a great bronze key with an ivory handle. Calling her maids to accompany her, she climbed up to a dark cavernous room where the armour of Odysseus, and of his father before him, was kept. The once gleaming shields and spears were now tarnished and the leather mouldy. She lifted from a wall the huge bow that belonged to Odysseus. The sight of it made her weep bitterly. She carried the bow and a quiver full of deadly arrows to the hall. Her maids followed with a box full of iron and bronze axes.

The suitors were lounging in the hall as usual. Penelope addressed them in a steady voice. 'Whoever can string this bow and shoot

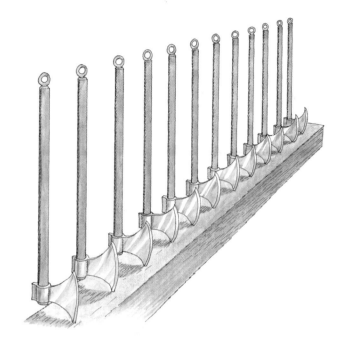

an arrow through the rings of these twelve axes – that man I will marry.' Then Telemachus stood the axes in a row with their handles in the air, so that the rings on the handle ends by which they hung on the wall were all aligned.

A suitor seized the bow and strained with all his might to bend the arc of wood. It was useless; he did not have the strength. Others came up but none could string the bow, though they strained till their hands bled. Antinous hung back, for he feared to fail. 'The bow is dry and hard,' he said, 'bring tallow from the storehouse to grease the wood.' He melted the animal fat and greased the bow, turning it round in front of the fire to warm it, and then he tried to string it. But although he was the strongest amongst them he could not bend the bow.

Odysseus in his beggar's disguise had sat to one side. Now came the opportunity that Athene had promised. He stretched out his hand for the bow. 'May an old man be allowed to try?' he asked. 'I'm not competing for a wife. I only want to see what strength I have left after all my sufferings.'

The suitors roared with laughter, but Telemachus stepped in to silence them. 'All guests in my hall shall be treated with respect,' he said. 'Give the old man the bow.'

Then, after so many years, Odysseus once more stroked his well-loved bow. As easily as a musician stretches a new string to a lyre he strung the mighty bow, without effort or hurry. Then with his right hand he tested the string and it sang as he plucked it. The

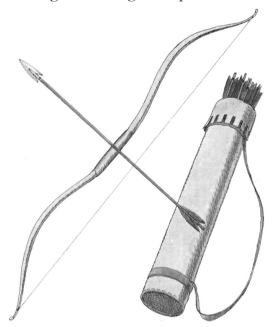

suitors watched, humiliated. Then the colour drained from their faces for before their eyes the stooping beggar became a powerful, angry king. He took an arrow from the quiver and, without rising from the stool, shot it directly through the row of axe-rings.

Then he called to his son. 'Telemachus,

the time has come to give these suitors the feast that they deserve.' He leapt to his feet and stood across the entrance to the hall with the bow in his hands and the full quiver at his side.

'You dogs!' Odysseus cried. 'You never thought to see me back from Troy. You robbed my household, misused my people, oppressed my wife - as though there were no gods in Olympus. One and all, your fate is sealed.' Then he let loose a rain of arrows. The first to fall was Antinous, pierced through the throat. Then there was uproar. The suitors tried in vain to escape; they could not, for Odysseus blocked the doorway. Soon, all lay dead. Odysseus was in possession of the hall, the palace and the kingdom.

The only thing still to be retaken was the heart of Penelope. She could scarcely believe that this figure, so much older and more careworn, was the young husband of her memories. Odysseus saw her hesitation. 'I can sleep here in the hall,' he said.

Then Penelope knew how to test him. 'I will have the great bed brought from my room and set up in the hall for you,' she said.

'What are you saying?' cried Odysseus. 'How can the bed be moved? With my own hands I built our marriage chamber around a living olive tree, and shaped its trunk to be a bedpost for our bed. Who has dared to cut that trunk and move the bed?' Then Penelope trembled and her heart melted, for no one but herself and her husband knew this secret. She threw her arms around Odysseus's neck. His homecoming was complete.

IN CASE YOU WERE WONDERING . . .

. . . **what goes on in a forge (page 9).**
A forge is a smith's workplace where he heats pieces of metal in a fierce fire, to make them soft enough to hammer into shape. The god Hephaestus was a smith, the first in the world according to the ancient Greeks.

. . . **what sort of plant fennel is (page 9).**
It is a Mediterranean herb which the Romans introduced to other lands. It tastes aniseed like and has masses of tiny yellow flowers on tall stalks which turn dry and hollow when the flowers go to seed.

. . . **what a bodkin is (page 17).**
A bodkin is a thick, blunt-ended needle. Arachne is saying, in the rudest way, that she doesn't need to ask Athene for the smallest favour.

. . . **what a shuttle is like (page 19).**
It is a weaving tool shaped like a squat, oval-ended spool, that carries the weft (the thread to be woven across the loom). As the weaver tosses the shuttle to and fro through the upright threads it draws the weft thread into place between them. According to the Roman poet Ovid, Athene had a shuttle of boxwood (the wood of the box tree). Boxwood, being very hard, could be smooth-polished to glide through the threads.

. . . **what an oracle was (page 28, 34, 72).**
A sacred place where a god was believed to answer questions. It might be a temple, a cave or a sacred grove. There was an oracle of Zeus at Dodona, in northern Greece, where he was supposed to speak through the rustling of oak leaves, but usually a priest or priestess spoke on behalf of a god, by going into a trance and uttering words as if inspired. One of the most famous oracles

was Apollo's at Delphi, on the spot where he was said to have killed the Python.

. . . **what type of cow a heifer is (page 34).**
A young cow that has not yet had a calf.

. . . **what a distaff is (page 37).**
A stick about a metre long, cleft at the top to hold a mass of raw (unspun) wool or flax. The spinner holds the distaff in one hand and draws fibres from it with the other, twisting them all the while to form a continuous thread.

. . . **about the Golden Fleece (page 47).**
The Fleece came from a magical golden ram which Zeus sent to rescue Phrixus, a prince of Thebes, whose stepmother was plotting to have him killed. The ram carried him over the sea to Colchis where he sacrificed it to Zeus in gratitude, and presented its fleece to King Aeetes.

. . . **what shades were (page 52).**
They were the spirits of the dead in the underworld. The ancient Greeks believed that after death people looked and behaved like shadows ('shades') of their living selves. Those that had led a good life went to the Elysian Fields, a pleasant part of the underworld.

. . . **why Theseus was unknown to his father (page 64).**
To protect him from plotting relatives, Theseus had been born secretly in a distant city. Before leaving his baby son, Aegeus had hidden a sword and pair of sandals under a rock and told Theseus's mother not to let the boy come to Athens until he was strong enough to lift the rock and take the sword and sandals.

INDEX